What the Critics Have ... *Wollstone-craft and* A VINDICATION OF THE RIGHTS OF WOMAN

"... a philosophizing serpent . . . hyena in petticoats."
Horace Walpole, *Letters*, 1792 [1905]

"... every one declares it is the most indecent Rhapsody that ever was penned by man or woman." Eliza Bishop (Mary W.'s sister), letter to Everina Wollstonecraft (her other sister), 1793

" . . . when we consider the importance of its doctrines, and the eminence of genius it displays, it seems not very improbable that it will be read as long as the English language endures." William Godwin, *Memoirs*, 1798

". . . the world was not worthy of her. . . . In loftiness of spirit, decisiveness of character, clearness of intellect, purity of intention, and benevolence of heart, the great Luminary of Heaven never yet shed his beams on a human creature superior to Mary Wollstonecraft Godwin." Anonymous, *A Defence of the Character and Conduct of the Late Mary Wollstonecraft Godwin, founded on principles of Nature and Reason, as applied to the Peculiar Circumstances of her Case, in a Series of Letters to A Lady*, 1803

"It has, by turns, pleased and displeased, startled and half-convinced me that its author is oftener right than wrong."
Anna Seward, *Letters*, 1811

"The book which made her [Wollstonecraft's] name famous . . . won for her then, as it has done since, an admiration from half of mankind only equalled by the reprobation of the other half. Yet most of its theories, then considered so dangerously extreme, would to-day be contested by few." Mrs. Julian Marshall, *The Life & Letters of Mary Wollstonecraft Shelley*, 1889

"What was absolutely new in the world's history was that for the first time a woman dared to sit down to write a book which was not an echo of men's thinking . . . but a first exploration of the problems of society and morals from a standpoint which recognised humanity without ignoring sex. She showed her genius not so much in writing the book, which is, indeed, a faulty though an intensely vital performance, as in thinking out its position for herself. . . . The miracle was that Mary Wollstonecraft's mind was never distorted by bitterness, nor her faith in mankind destroyed by cynicism." H. N. Brailsford, *Shelley, Godwin, and Their Circle*, 1913

"Mary Wollstonecraft has her place in history as the great pioneer of the feminist movement. . . . The ideals she set have never been surmounted and no modern programme of advancement has passed the aim that she in her darkness saw shining far ahead." Madeline Linford, *Mary Wollstonecraft*, 1924

". . . as challenging to-day as in the day in which it was written—and far more likely now to be understood. . . . the sincerity which shines through its laboured phrases redeems at once the pretentiousness and the crudity of this pamphlet. . . . It is among the sane fanatics that Mary Wollstonecraft claims her place." George E. G. Catlin, Introduction to Everyman Edition, 1929

"Though *The Rights of Woman* has few striking literary qualities of its own, it stands as a landmark in the path of literary development: it adumbrated, without respect to class or caste, the social and intellectual equality of the sexes which was before long to effect a revolution in literature through the multiplication of books by women writers." A. C. Ward, *English Literature*, 1958

". . . the best of it sounds loud and clear, an inspiration still powerful in an age when human rights are a daily concern. . . . What gives her book its timeless appeal is not primarily the originality or the profundity of her ideas (for they have neither), nor the eloquence of her prose (which is not always eloquent), but her devotion to her fellow men and her concern for their well being." Charles W. Hagelman, Jr., Introduction to Norton paperback edition, 1967

"What is so astonishing about the *Vindication* is not that Mary wrote it, but that she was alone in raising the issues that she did, in a period of social change. . . . we know that Mary Wollstonecraft wrote a classic whose seminal influence on the social history of women has no equal." Eleanor Flexner, *Mary Wollstonecraft*, 1972

"Her temperament greatly resembled that of Peanuts' Lucy. . . . This characteristic, coupled with her alarming energy and forcefulness, made her redoubtable indeed." Arthur M. Wilson, *The New York Times Book Review*, 1975

"It was a stroke of genius to associate rights of man with women's subjugation; it took brilliant courage and originality to explode ageless tradition. . . . Mary Wollstonecraft faced universal feminine and human problems, viewed them freshly, and assaulted them with insistent passion, originality, and optimism. Her essential insights have been rediscovered, often independently, and acted on in subsequent generations." Emily Sunstein, *A Different Face*, 1975

". . . I will not characterize her neatly as one kind or another of political or feminist theorist. It is considerably more important and interesting to show the range of ways in which her work was related to other themes, traditions, and theorists. . . . to recognize the ways in which she reached her own conclusions and syntheses, which are not summarized adequately by partisan labels." Virginia Sapiro, *A Vindication of Political Virtue*, 1992

Ahead of Her Time

A *SAMPLER* OF THE *LIFE* AND *THOUGHT*

of

MARY WOLLSTONECRAFT

Ahead of Her Time

A *SAMPLER* OF THE *LIFE* AND *THOUGHT*

of

MARY WOLLSTONECRAFT

Being Excerpts from her Letters and Writings on
WOMEN'S RIGHTS; THE RIGHTS OF MAN; THE FRENCH REVOLUTION;
EDUCATION; MORAL VALUES; THE SLAVERY OF MARRIAGE; SOCIAL
JUSTICE; WEALTH AND POVERTY; THE EVILS OF POWER AND
PROPERTY; THE VENALITY OF POLITICIANS;
And Her Own Account of
Her Struggle for Independence; Her Unconventional Life;
Her Ill-Fated Liaison with Gilbert Imlay; and Her Finding Happiness
at Last with William Godwin before Her Early Death Following the
Birth of her Daughter Mary, the Future Author of *Frankenstein.*

Selected and Arranged by
ELLA MAZEL

BERNEL BOOKS / LARCHMONT, NEW YORK

Designed by Ella Mazel, with border and ornaments
reproduced from 18th century volumes.

Excerpts from the letters have been gleaned from
The Collected Letters of Mary Wollstonecraft, the definitive volume
by Ralph Wardle (Cornell University Press, 1979).

The following are gratefully acknowledged
as the holders of the original letters:

THE CARL H. PFORZHEIMER COLLECTION OF SHELLEY AND HIS CIRCLE
The New York Public Library
Astor, Lenox and Tilden Foundations
for those addressed to Jane Arden, Ruth Barlow (1793), George Dyson,
Reverend Gabell, Mary Hays, and Joseph Johnson;

LORD ABINGER (whose collection is on long-term loan
to the Bodleian Library, Oxford), for those addressed to George Blood,
William Godwin, and Eliza and Everina Wollstonecraft;

LIVERPOOL CENTRAL LIBRARIES for those addressed to William Roscoe;

THE BANCROFT LIBRARY OF THE UNIVERSITY OF CALIFORNIA AT BERKELEY
for those addressed to Ruth Barlow in 1794.

Library of Congress Cataloging-in-Publication Data

Wollstonecraft, Mary, 1759-1797.
Ahead of her time : a sampler of the life and thought of Mary Wollstonecraft / selected and arranged by Ella Mazel.
p. cm.
"Being excerpts from her letters and writings on women's rights; the
rights of man; the French Revolution; education; moral values; the slavery
of marriage; social justice; wealth and poverty; the evils of power and
property; the venality of politicians; and her own account of her struggle
for independence; her unconventional life; her ill-fated liaison with Gilbert
Imlay; and her finding happiness at last with William Godwin before her
early death following the birth of her daughter Mary, the future author of
Frankenstein."
Includes bibliographical references.
ISBN 0-9641887-3-2 (pbk.)
1. Wollstonecraft, Mary, 1759-1797. 2. Women authors, English--
18th century--Biography. 3. Feminists--Great Britain--Biography. 4.
Social problems. 5. Women's rights. 6. Feminism.
I. Title.
PR5841.W8Z476 1995
823'.7--dc20
[B]
95-41457
CIP

Published by Bernel Books, Box 419, Larchmont, NY 10538
Distributed by Brunner/Mazel, Inc.
19 Union Square West, New York NY 10003

To the young and youngest women in my life

— two daughters, two daughters-in-law,

and five granddaughters —

who are not "hapless" thanks to Mary Wollstonecraft

and the long line of women's rights "champions"

who have helped make her dream a reality for them.

———————————

To the four young men who have supported them,

in the best feminist sense, all the way.

———————————

And to my husband, who in the course of fifty-three years

has learned at his peril not to open doors for me

that I can open for myself.

Contents

Introduction

First things first. Mary Wollstonecraft is not the author of *Frankenstein*. That was her daughter, Mary Wollstonecraft Shelley. And that's another story.

This Mary Wollstonecraft lives on because, two hundred years ago, she wrote a revolutionary book called *A Vindication of the Rights of Woman*—for which she has been variously rejected, respected, or neglected, depending on one's point of view. Interest in her has revived, however, with every new cycle in the feminist movement. A paperback edition of *Vindication* was issued in 1967, and in the 1970s alone, with the blossoming of the contemporary "women's lib" movement, there appeared three full-scale biographies, an anthology of her writings, and a collection of her letters.

Wollstonecraft is a major figure in what has been called "women's studies," and a great deal of scholarly analysis and interpretation is being devoted to her role in this area. But a reading of *Vindication*, along with her other published writings and her letters, reveals an awesome breadth of insight into the root causes of the plight not only of women, but of society as a whole.

And this insight need not be the exclusive domain of scholars or feminists, nor relegated to the mists of history. At its core are reflections and opinions that, grounded though they are in the particular circumstances of her time, speak eloquently to those who today are wrestling with similar problems, whether in human rights, in the disparity between rich and poor, in the demagoguery of politicians, or in education.

All of Wollstonecraft's works are currently available —in fact, a complete set of her writings, in seven volumes, was published in 1994. Unfortunately, they are hard for the modern reader to deal with. Even an admirer like H. N. Brailsford wrote, in 1913, that *Vindication* "is ill-arranged, full of repetitions, full of digressions, and almost without a regular plan. Its style is unformed, sometimes rhetorical, sometimes familiar.

"But with all these faults, it teems with apt phrases, telling passages, vigorous sentences which sum up in a few convincing lines the substance of its message."

And that is the raison d'être of this little volume—to convey "the substance of its message" by selecting and arranging those "apt phrases" and "telling passages" from Wollstonecraft's letters and writings that are still relevant two hundred years later.

In transcribing the passages, I have taken some liberties with the originals, for Wollstonecraft was notoriously careless with her punctuation and spelling. In order for her meaning to be easy to grasp and unambiguous, I have, for example, added or deleted commas and semicolons as necessary. At the same time, I have retained the original spelling—as in "shew" for "show"—where it does not interfere with the flow of the thought. And I have, as do all who quote from Wollstonecraft, made generous use of ellipses (. . .) to represent the omission of words, phrases, sentences, or even paragraphs—being careful, of course, to retain the sense of the original while ensuring that each extract flows smoothly.

In the context of this book as a "sampler," information about Mary Wollstonecraft's life and times is spread over the various chapters in the form of brief introductions. These are supplemented by a chronology, a bibliography, and information about the individuals to whom her letters are addressed.

For the most part, her own writing speaks for itself.

Any contemporary anthology of women's history, philosophy, politics, or sociology invariably includes either a tribute to Wollstonecraft or a contribution from her . . . She welded the connection between the ideals of social revolution and her original intuitive awareness of women's need to rise from their degraded status, a connection that remains firm down to our own times.

Moira Ferguson and Janet Todd
Mary Wollstonecraft, 1984

A brief chronology

NOTE: The names of places from which
Wollstonecraft's letters were sent
are <u>underlined</u>.

1759   Born April 2, the second of six children, the place of her birth not definitely known

1768   Family relocates in town of <u>Beverley</u> in Yorkshire

1775   Meets Fanny Blood, an older girl whom Mary decides she would like to spend her life with

1778   Works as companion to a Mrs. Dawson, spends time in <u>Bath</u>, <u>Windsor</u>, and Southampton

1782   Goes home to nurse mother, who dies April 19; her sister Eliza marries Meredith Bishop in <u>Bermondsey</u> in October; Mary goes to live with Fanny Blood's family in <u>Walham Green</u>

1784   Called back to <u>Bermondsey</u> to tend Eliza, Mary takes her away with her to <u>Hackney</u> and Islington, where, with Fanny, they set up a school; lacking success, they start another one in <u>Newington Green</u>

1785   Fanny Blood leaves for Lisbon in February to marry Hugh Skeys, dies in childbirth in November with Mary in attendance

1786   School having failed, Mary returns to London, writes *Thoughts on the Education of Daught-*

ers; goes to work as governess for Lord and Lady Kingsborough in Mitchelstown, Ireland, also spends time with them in Eton, Dublin and Bristol

1787   Dismissed from post in August; visits her sister Everina, who is teaching school in Henley; goes to stay with publisher Joseph Johnson in London

1788   Works for Johnson on translations, and writing articles for *Analytical Review*; novel, *Mary*, and *Original Stories from Real Life* published

1790   Spends a few weeks in August and September with Henry Gabell and his wife in Warminster; *A Vindication of the Rights of Men* published anonymously in December

1791   Second edition published, under her name; in October, starts writing *Woman*, poses for portrait requested by William Roscoe; in November, meets William Godwin, who has begun his *Political Justice*

1792   *A Vindication of the Rights of Woman* published; meets Mary Hays; Gilbert Imlay publishes *A Topographical Description of the Western Territory of Northern America*; Mary goes to Paris in December

1793   Godwin's *Political Justice* published; Mary meets Gilbert Imlay, his *The Emigrants* published in London; moves to Neuilly-sur-Seine in June, becomes pregnant in August, returns to Paris; registers as Imlay's wife at U.S. embassy in September

1794   Baby, named Fanny after Mary's friend, born
        May 14 in <u>Le Havre</u>; in August, Imlay goes
        to Paris and London, Mary spends fall and
        winter in <u>Paris</u>; *An Historical and Moral
        View of the Origin and Progress of the
        French Revolution* published

1795   After a brief time in Havre, makes unsuccessful
        suicide attempt in <u>London</u>; from June to
        September, travels in Scandinavia as Imlay's
        agent, making stops in <u>Hull</u> on the way there
        and <u>Hamburg</u> on the way back; in <u>London</u> in
        October, is rescued from Thames in second
        suicide attempt

1796   *Letters Written during a Short Residence in Swe-
        den, Norway, and Denmark* published; calls
        on Godwin, they become lovers; becomes
        pregnant in December

1797   Marries Godwin on March 29; gives birth August
        30 to a daughter, Mary; dies September 10

Ahead of Her Time

A *SAMPLER* OF THE *LIFE* AND *THOUGHT*

of

MARY WOLLSTONECRAFT

Part One

THE WOMAN

According to H. R. James in *Mary Wollstone-craft—A Sketch*, "she is herself greater than her works. Her writings, including the famous *Vindication*, have a singular interest through the revelation which they make of herself; and this personal interest is sometimes stronger than the literary.

"For in her books, and still more in her letters, is a wealth of biographical material, out of which . . . emerges the portrait of a woman of rare gifts and powers, intellectually, emotionally, physically; a woman of strong understanding and of indomitable will; above all, of a woman most lovable, endowed with a great power of loving and of rendering service to those she loved. . . . Mary Wollstonecraft, the daughter, sister, lover, wife, and mother, is even more admirable than Mary Wollstonecraft, the pioneer woman of letters."

It therefore seems fitting that we become acquainted with the woman before getting into the essence of her work.

. . . those whom curiosity prompted to
seek the occasion of beholding her, expected to find a sturdy, muscular, raw-
boned virago; and they were not a little
surprised, when, instead of all this, they
found a woman, lovely in her person,
and, in the best and most engaging sense,
feminine in her manners.

William Godwin, *Memoirs*, 1798

Self-Portrait

From the very first entry, written when she was fourteen, it is clear that Wollstonecraft was a most extraordinary young woman. Her "peculiar bent" and "active mind" are evident in both her correspondence and her published work, as she struggles for freedom and independence, not only for herself, but for all whom she considers equally enslaved.

I have a heart that scorns disguise, and a countenance which will not dissemble:—I have formed romantic notions of friendship.—I have been once disappointed:—I think if I am a second time I shall only want some infidelity in a love affair, to qualify me for an old maid . . . I am a little singular in my thoughts of love and friendship; I must have the first place or none. [Letter to Jane Arden: Beverley, ca 1773-4]

The more I see of the world, the more anxious I am to preserve my old friends, for I am now slower than ever in forming friendships; I would wish to cherish a universal love to all mankind, but the principal part of my heart must be occupied by those who have for years had a place there. [Letter to Jane Arden: Bath, ca December 1779-January 1780]

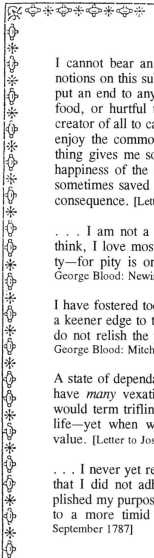

I cannot bear an unfeeling mortal:—Indeed I carry my notions on this subject a great way:— I think it murder to put an end to any living thing unless it be necessary for food, or hurtful to us.—If it has pleased the beneficent creator of all to call them into being, we ought to let them enjoy the common blessings of nature, and I declare no thing gives me so much pleasure as to contribute to the happiness of the most insignificant creature . . . I have sometimes saved the life of a fly, and thought myself of consequence. [Letter to Jane Arden: Windsor, June-August 1780]

. . . I am not a fair-weather friend—on the contrary, I think, I love most people best when they are in adversity—for pity is one of my prevailing passions. [Letter to George Blood: Newington Green, July 1785]

I have fostered too great a refinement of mind, and given a keener edge to the sensibility nature gave me—so that I do not relish the pleasures most people pursue. [Letter to George Blood: Mitchelstown, December 1786]

A state of dependance must ever be irksome to me, and I have *many* vexations to encounter, which some people would term trifling—I have most of the . . . comforts of life—yet when weighed with liberty they are of little value. [Letter to Joseph Johnson: Mitchelstown, December 1786]

. . . I never yet resolved to do any thing of consequence, that I did not adhere resolutely to it, till I had accomplished my purpose, improbable as it might have appeared to a more timid mind. [Letter to Joseph Johnson: Henley, September 1787]

. . . I am not born to tread in the beaten track—the peculiar bent of my nature pushes me on. [Letter to Everina: London, November 1787]

I cannot bear to do any thing I cannot do well—and I should lose time in the vain attempt. [Letter to Joseph Johnson: London, 1787-8]

. . . sheer love of knowledge . . . has ever been a pre-dominate mover in my little world. [Letter to Everina: London, March 1788]

Blessed be that Power who gave me an active mind! if it does not smooth, it enables me to jump over the rough places in life. [Letter to George Blood: London, February 1789]

Independence I have long considered as the grand blessing of life, the basis of every virtue—and independence I will ever secure by contracting my wants, though I were to live on a barren heath. [*Rights of Woman*, 1792]

Thanks to that Being who . . . gave me sufficient strength of mind to dare to exert my own reason, till . . . I view, with indignation, the mistaken notions that enslave my sex. [*Rights of Woman*, 1792]

I am a mere animal, and instinctive emotions too often silence the suggestions of reason. . . . I am a strange compound of weakness and resolution! — However, if I must suffer, I will endeavour to suffer in silence. There is certainly a great defect in my mind—my wayward heart creates its own misery— Why I am made thus I cannot

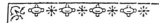

tell; and, till I can form some idea of the whole of my existence, I must be content to weep and dance like a child—long for a toy, and be tired of it as soon as I get it.
[Letter to Joseph Johnson: London, ca late 1792]

. . . when I follow the lead of my heart . . . my mind has always hitherto enabled my body to do whatever I wished.
[Letter to Imlay: Paris, January 1794]

[Beverley] appeared so diminutive; and, when I found that many of the inhabitants had lived in the same houses ever since I left it, I could not help wondering how they could thus have vegetated, whilst I was running over a world of sorrow, snatching at pleasure, and throwing off prejudices.
[Letter to Imlay: Hull, June 1795]

For years have I endeavoured to calm an impetuous tide—labouring to make my feelings take an orderly course.—It was striving against the stream.—I must love and admire with warmth, or I sink into sadness. [*Short Residence*, 1795]

What a long time it requires to know ourselves; and yet almost every one has more of this knowledge than he is willing to own, even to himself. I cannot immediately determine whether I ought to rejoice at having turned over . . . a new page in the history of my own heart. [*Short Residence*, 1795]

. . . I have a spirit that will never bend, or take indirect methods, to obtain the consequence I despise; nay, if to support life it was necessary to act contrary to my principles, the struggle would soon be over. I can bear any thing but my own contempt. [Letter to ————: London, late 1795]

Those who are bold enough to advance before the age they live in, and to throw off, by the force of their own minds, the prejudices which the maturing reason of the world will in time disavow, must learn to brave censure. We ought not to be too anxious respecting the opinion of others. [Letter to Mary Hays(?): London, summer 1797]

Tribulations

Here we follow Wollstonecraft from the age of twenty, when she started supporting herself as a paid companion, to twenty-eight, when she was poised to become a full-time writer.

They reflect her bitterness—over her father's alcoholism and irresponsibility, her mother's helplessness and alienation, the death in childbirth of a beloved friend, and the burden of taking responsibility for her younger sisters and brothers—her ill health, and her sense of resignation and despair.

It was during this time, however, that she wrote her first book, in spite of all her "misfortunes and vexations." The manuscript, entitled THOUGHTS ON THE EDUCATION OF DAUGHTERS, brought her to the attention of Joseph Johnson, the London publisher who was to become her mentor and father-figure.

I often recollect with pleasure the many agreeable days we spent together when we eagerly told every girlish secret of our hearts—Those were peaceful days;—yours since that period may have been as tranquil, but mine have been far otherwise. [Letter to Jane Arden: Bath, ca May-June, 1779]

. . . my father's violent temper, and extravagant turn of mind, was the principal cause of my unhappiness and that of the rest of my family . . . . his passions were seldom directed at me, yet I suffered more than any of them—my spirits were weak—in short, a lingering sickness was the consequence of it, and if my constitution had not been very strong, I must have fallen a sacrifice long before this. [Letter to Jane Arden: Bath, ca May-June 1779]

. . . you don't say a word of my mother, I take it for granted she is well—tho' of late she has not even desired to be remembered to me.—Some time or the other, in this world or a better, she may be convinced of my regard—and then may think I deserve not to be thought so harshly of. [Letter to Eliza: Windsor, August 1780]

. . . time has blunted the edge of many vexations that I once thought I could never bear—I have no hope nor do I endeavor to attain any thing but composure of mind, and that I expect to gain in some degree in spite of the storms and cross winds of life. [Letter to Everina: Bermondsey, ca late 1783]

I have been very ill . . . have been bled and blistered—yet still I am not well— My harrassed mind will in time wear out my body—I have been so hunted down by cares . . . that my spirits are quite depressed—I have lost all relish for life and my broken heart is only cheared by the prospect of death—I may be years a-dying tho' and so I ought to be patient—for at this time to wish myself away would be selfish. [Letter to George Blood: Newington Green, July 1785]

I by no means like the proposal of being a governess—I should be shut out from society—and be debarred the *imperfect* pleasures of friendship—as I should on every side be surrounded by *unequals*— To live only on terms of civility and common benevolence without any interchange of little acts of kindness and tenderness would be to me extremely irksome. [Letter to George Blood: Newington Green, July 1786]

There was such a solemn kind of stupidity about this place as froze my very blood— I entered the great gates with the same kind of feeling as I should have if I was going into the Bastile . . . I am however treated like a gentlewoman by every part of the family—but the forms and parade of high life suit not my mind— I am in a land of strangers. [Letter to Everina: Mitchelstown, October 1786]

. . . my spirits have been in continual agitation—and when they will be at rest, heaven only knows! I fear I am not equal to the tasks I have been persuaded to undertake—and this fear worries me . . . . I have scarcely a moment to myself to collect my thought and *reason* sorrow away— when I am alone I endeavour to study the french—and this unwearied application to business undermines my health. [Letter to Eliza: Mitchelstown, November 1786]

. . . mine, at present, might be termed comparative rather than positive misery—let it be called what it will—I am grown a poor melancholy wretch . . . . If my vanity could be flattered by the respect of people whose judgement I do not care a fig for—why in this place it has sufficient food . . . . [I] am wonderfully entertaining and then I retire to

my room, form figures in the fire, listen to the wind . . .
and so does time *waste* away in apathy or misery. [Letter
to Everina: Mitchelstown, November 1786]

I am, at present, rather melancholy than unhappy—the
things of this world appear *flat, stale* and *unprofitable* to
me . . . a listless kind of despair has taken possession of
me, which I cannot shake off; however, I am satisfied,
and will try contentedly to travel through the *solitary* path
fate has thrown me into. [Letter to Everina: Dublin, March
1787]

Confined almost entirely to the society of children, I am
anxiously solicitous for their future welfare, and mortified
beyond measure, when counteracted in my endeavours to
improve them.—I feel all a mother's fears for the swarm
of little ones which surround me, and observe disorders,
without having the power to apply the proper remedies.
[Letter to Joseph Johnson: Dublin, April 1787]

"That vivacity which increases with age is not far from
madness". . . I then am mad—deprived of the only
comforts I can relish, I give way to whim—and yet when
the most sprightly sallies burst from me the tear frequently
trembles in my eye and the long drawn sigh eases my full
heart. [Letter to Everina: Dublin, May 1787]

. . . I have been in every respect very unfortunate: indeed
from my infancy I have drank of the bitter cup, my
fortune has not been chequered, on the contrary one color
has prevailed, and given its tincture to my frame of
mind—the *tone* of melancholy you observed on our first

acquaintance. . . . were I to give you an account of *all* my misfortunes, and vexations, I should write a volume instead of a letter. [Letter to Reverend Gabell: Henley, September 1787]

Independence

At last, Wollstonecraft was in a position to pursue a literary career under Johnson's aegis (more about this under "*Author*"). In London, she became part of a stimulating intellectual circle that included Samuel Johnson and Thomas Paine. During the next five years she was to produce her major works.

Finally, she made her much-longed-for trip to France, where, as she was to write jokingly, "I might take a husband for the time being."

I often think of my new plan of life . . . I am determined! . . . I long for a little peace and *independence*! Every obligation we receive from our fellow-creatures is a new shackle, takes from our native freedom, and debases the mind, makes us mere earthworms—I am not fond of grovelling! [Letter to Joseph Johnson: Henley, September 1787]

I *have* left Lord K's . . . You can conceive how disagreeable pity and advice would be at this juncture. . . . My undertaking would subject me to ridicule—and an *inundation* of *friendly* advice, to which I cannot listen. . . . when I *reflect* on past mercies with respect to the future I am not without hope— And freedom—*even* uncertain freedom—is dear. [Letter to Everina: London, September 1787]

I informed Mr Johnson of my situation: he insisted on my coming to his house, and contrived to detain me there a long time—you can *scarcely* conceive how warmly, and delicately he has interested himself in my fate. He has now settled me in a little house . . . All this will appear to you like a a dream; whenever I am tired of solitude I go to Mr Johnson's, and there I meet the kind of company *I* find most pleasure in. [Letter to Everina: London, November 1787]

. . . I am studying French, and wish I had an opportunity of conversing—indeed, if I have ever any money to spare to gratify myself, I will certainly visit France. It has long been a desire floating in my brain, that even hope has not given *consistency* to; and yet it does not evaporate. [Letter to Everina: London, March 1788]

I have lately been very busy translating a work of importance, and have made a very advantageous contract for another . . . in short . . . I succeed beyond my most sanguine hopes. . . . I have determined on one thing, *never* to have my Sisters to live with me, my solitary manner of living would not suit them, nor *could* I pursue my studies if forced to conform. [Letter to George Blood: London, May 1788]

. . . my die is cast.—I could not now resign intellectual pursuits for domestic comforts—and yet I think I could form an idea of more *elegant* felicity—where mind chastens sensation, and rational converse gave a little dignity to fondness. [Letter to Everina: Warminster, September 1790]

. . . be it known unto you that my book &c &c has afforded me an opportunity of settling *very* advantageous in the matrimonial line, with a new acquaintance; but entre nous—a handsome house and a proper man did not tempt me. [Letter to Everina: London, February 1792]

I intend . . . to set out for Paris in the course of a fortnight or three weeks . . . I am told the world . . . married me to him [Johnson] . . . but . . . I am still a Spinster on the wing. At Paris, indeed, I might take a husband for the time being, and get divorced when my truant heart longed again to nestle with its old friends; but this speculation has not yet entered into my plan. [Letter to William Roscoe: London, November 1792]

I am almost overwhelmed with civility here, and have even met with more than civility. [Letter to Ruth Barlow: Paris, February 1793]

Imlay

The "more than civility" in the previous passage probably refers to the beginning of Wollstonecraft's relationship with Gilbert Imlay, the American entrepreneur she met in Paris. She loved him with total abandon, but he was not ready for the life of domestic felicity she yearned for. Instead, they spent far less time together than they did apart, while he made frequent trips in pursuit of what she saw as the chimerical goal of financial success.

It's quite possible that her scolding may have helped drive him away, but the duplicity of his living with a mistress, while assuring Mary of his devotion to her and their daughter, does not encourage one to believe that he was the man she wanted him to be.

So anxious was she to hold on to Imlay that, after her first aborted suicide attempt in May 1795, Mary—with daughter and maid in tow—traveled to Scandinavia as his agent. Amazingly, at the same time that she was sending him some of her most desperate appeals, she was able to draft the vivid and insightful descriptions of her travels that would be published a year later as LETTERS WRITTEN DURING A SHORT RESIDENCE IN SWEDEN, NORWAY, AND DENMARK.

"Pathetic and lonely," wrote Roger Ingpen in his preface to *The Love Letters of Mary Wollstonecraft to Gilbert Imlay*, "she . . . will continue to evoke sympathy when her books are no longer read. . . . Other writers have been unhappy and have known the pains of unrequited love, but Mary Wollstonecraft addressed these letters with a breaking heart to the man whom she adored, the most passionate love letters in our literature."

The final breakup does not come till after a protracted series of "last" letters and a second suicide attempt.

You can scarcely imagine with what pleasure I anticipate the day, when we are to begin almost to live together. . . Cherish me with that dignified tenderness, which I have only found in you . . . and whilst you love me, I cannot again fall into the miserable state which rendered life a burthen almost too heavy to be borne. . . we are soon to meet, to try whether we have mind enough to keep our hearts warm. [Paris, August 1793]

Of late we are always separating. . . though I began to write cheerfully, some melancholy tears have found their way into my eyes, that linger there, whilst a glow of tenderness at my heart whispers that you are one of the best creatures in the world. . . . When we are settled in the country together . . . my heart . . . will learn to rest on yours, with that dignity your character, not to talk of my own, demands. [Paris, September 1793]

Ever since you last saw me inclined to faint, I have felt
some gentle twitches, which make me begin to think that
I am nourishing a creature who will soon be sensible of
my care.— This thought has not only produced an overflowing of tenderness to you, but made me very attentive
to calm my mind and take exercise, lest I should destroy
an object in whom we are to have a mutual interest. [Paris,
November 1793]

I do not know why, but I have more confidence in your
affection, when absent, than present; nay, I think that you
must love me, for, in the sincerity of my heart let me say
it, I believe I deserve your tenderness, because I am true,
and have a degree of sensibility that you can see and
relish. [Paris, December 1793]

I do not want to be loved like a goddess, but I wish to be
necessary to you. [Paris, January 1794]

. . . let me, in the sincerity of my heart, assure you, there
is nothing I would not suffer to make you happy. My own
happiness wholly depends on you; and, knowing you,
when my reason is not clouded, I look forward to a
rational prospect of as much felicity as the earth affords
with a little dash of rapture into the bargain, if you look
at me, when we meet again, as you have sometimes
greeted your humbled, yet most affectionate   Mary.
[Paris, January 1794]

I shall probably receive a letter from you to-day, sealing
my pardon—and I will be careful not to torment you with
my querulous humours . . . . What a picture have you

sketched of our fireside! Yes, my love, my fancy was instantly at work, and I found my head on your shoulder, whilst my eyes were fixed on the little creatures that were clinging about your knees. I did not absolutely determine that there should be six—if you have not set your heart on this round number. [Paris, January 1794]

Write often to your poor girl, and write long letters; for I not only like them for being longer, but because more heart steals into them; and I am happy to catch your heart whenever I can. [Paris, January 1794]

. . . I am to set out on Thursday . . . and hope to tell you soon (on your lips) how glad I shall be to see you. . . . I do not foresee any impediment to my reaching Havre, to bid you good night next Friday in my new apartment— where I am to meet you and love in spite of care, to smile me to sleep . . . . Let me indulge the thought that I have thrown out some tendrils to cling to the elm by which I wish to be supported.—This is talking a new language for me!—But, knowing that I am not a parasite-plant, I am willing to receive the proofs of affection, that every pulse replies to, when I think of being once more in the same house with you. [Paris, January 1794]

I am safe, through the protection of an American. A most worthy man, who joins to uncommon tenderness of heart and quickness of feeling, a soundness of understanding, and reasonableness of temper, rarely to be met with— Having also been brought up in the interiour parts of America, he is a most natural, unaffected creature. I am with him now at Havre, and shall remain there, till

circumstances point out what it is necessary for me to do.
[Letter to Everina: Havre, March 1794]

Teasing hinderance of one kind or other continually occur
to *us* here—you perceive that I am acquiring the matrimonial phraseology without having clogged my soul by
promising obedience &c &c. . . . I am still very well; but
imagine it cannot be long before this lively animal pops on
us. [Letter to Ruth Barlow: Havre, April 1794]

. . . I am . . . so well, that were it not for the inundation
of milk, which for the moment incommodes me, I could
forget the pain I endured six days ago— Yet nothing could
be more natural or easy than my labour . . . this struggle
of nature is rendered much more cruel by the ignorance
and affectation of women. . . . I have got a vigorous little
Girl, and you were so out in your calculation respecting
the quantity of brains she was to have, and the skull it
would require to contain them, that you made almost all
the caps so small I cannot use them . . . I feel great
pleasure at being a mother—and the constant tenderness of
my most affectionate companion makes me regard a fresh
tie as a blessing. . . . My little Girl begins to suck so
manfully that her father reckons saucily on her writing the
second part of the R——ts of Woman. [Letter to Ruth Barlow:
Havre, May 1794]

. . . I assure you that you are the friend of my bosom, and
the prop of my heart. [Havre, August 1794]

. . . you now and then wounded my sensibility, concealing
yourself till honest sympathy, giving you to me without

disguise, lets me look into a heart, which my half-broken one wishes to creep into, to be revived and cherished.—You have frankness of heart, but not often exactly that overflowing . . . which, becoming almost childish, appears a weakness only to the weak. [Havre, August 1794]

I have been playing and laughing with the little girl so long, that I cannot take up my pen to address you without emotion. Pressing her to my bosom, she looked so like you (*entre nous*, your best looks, for I do not admire your commercial face), every nerve seemed to vibrate to the touch, and I began to think that there was something in the assertion of man and wife being one—for you seemed to pervade my whole frame, quickening the beat of my heart, and lending me the sympathetic tears you excited. [Paris, September 1794]

It is a heartless task to write letters without knowing whether they will ever reach you. . . . After your return, I hope indeed that you will not be so immersed in business, as during the last three or four months past—for even money, taking into account all the future comforts it is to procure, may be gained at too dear a rate, if painful impressions are left on the mind. . . . I feel that I love you; and, if I cannot be happy with you, I will seek it nowhere else. [Paris, October 1794]

I want to be sure that you are safe—and not separated from me by a sea that must be passed. . . . Come to me, my dearest friend, husband, father of my child!—All these fond ties glow at my heart at this moment, and dim my eyes.—With you an independence is desirable; and it is always within our reach, if affluence escapes us—without you the world again appears empty to me. [Paris, December 1794]

I do not like this life of continual inquietude, and . . . I am determined to try to earn some money here myself, in order to convince you that, if you chuse to run about the world to get a fortune, it is for yourself—for the little girl and I will live without your assistance, unless you are with us. I may be termed proud—Be it so—but I will never abandon certain principles of action. . . . if a wandering of the heart, or even a caprice of the imagination detains you—there is an end of all my hopes of happiness.—I could not forgive it if I would. [Paris, December 1794]

Fatigued during my youth by the most arduous struggles . . . the most melancholy views of life were impressed by a disappointed heart on my mind. Since I knew you, I have . . . allowed some time to glide away, winged with the delight which only spontaneous enjoyment can give.— Why have you so soon dissolved the charm? . . . I do not chuse to be a secondary object.—If your feelings were in unison with mine, you would not sacrifice so much to visionary prospects of future advantage. [Paris, January 1795]

The melancholy presentiment has for some time hung on my spirits, that we were parted forever . . . so many feelings are struggling for utterance, and agitating a heart almost bursting with anguish, that I find it very difficult to write with any degree of coherence. . . . I did not expect this blow from you. . . . if I am not to have any return of affection to reward me, I have the sad consolation of knowing that I deserved a better fate. My soul is weary—I am sick at heart; and, but for this little darling, I would cease to care about a life, which is now stripped of every charm. . . . I wanted the support of your affection—that gone, all is over! . . . Perhaps this is the last letter you will ever receive from me. [Paris, February 1795]

You talk of "permanent views and future comfort"—not for me, for I am dead to hope. . . . my heart is not only broken, but my constitution destroyed. . . . For a year or two you may procure yourself what you call pleasure, but . . . in the solitude of declining life, I shall be remembered with regret. [Paris, February 1795]

Here I am . . . on the wing towards you . . . . I cannot indulge the very affectionate tenderness which glows in my bosom, without trembling, till I see, by your eyes, that it is mutual. [Havre, April 1795]

It seems to me that I have not only lost the hope, but the power, of being happy.—Every emotion is now sharpened by anguish. My soul has been shook, and my tone of feelings destroyed. . . . My friend—my dear friend—examine yourself well . . . and discover . . . whether you desire to live with me, or part for ever? When you can once ascertain it, tell me frankly, I conjure you! [London, May 1795]

. . . am I always to be tossed about thus?—shall I never find an asylum to rest *contented* in? How can you love to fly about continually—dropping down, as it were, in a new world—cold and strange!—every other day? Why do you not attach those tender emotions round the idea of home, which even now dim my eyes? [Hull, May-June 1795]

I shall always consider it as one of the most serious misfortunes of my life, that I did not meet you before satiety had rendered your senses so fastidious as almost to close up every tender avenue of sentiment and affection that leads to your sympathetic heart. You have a heart, my friend, yet, hurried away by the impetuosity of inferior feelings, you have sought in vulgar excesses for that gratification which only the heart can bestow. . . . Examine now yourself . . . consider whether you find it necessary to sacrifice me to what you term "the zest of life." [Hull, June 1795]

Accuse me not of pride—yet sometimes . . . I have wondered that you did not set a higher value on my heart. [Hull, June 1795]

. . . we must either resolve to live together, or part for ever, I cannot bear these continual struggles. [Sweden, July 1795]

I cannot tear my affections from you—and, though every remembrance stings me to the soul, I think of you till I make allowance for the very defects of character that have given such a cruel stab to my peace. . . . It is my misfortune that my imagination is perpetually shading your defects and lending you charms, whilst the grossness of your senses makes you (call me not vain) overlook graces in me, that only dignity of mind, and the sensibility of an expanded heart can give. [Sweden, July 1795]

Believe me, there is such a thing as a broken heart!
[Sweden, July 1795]

This state of suspense, my friend, is intolerable; we must
determine on something—and soon;—we must meet short-
ly, or part for ever. . . . I feel that I cannot endure the
anguish of corresponding with you—if we are only to
correspond.—No; if you seek for happiness elsewhere, my
letters shall not interrupt your repose. I will be dead to
you. [Norway, August 1795]

I am disgusted with myself for having so long importuned
you with my affection. [Norway, August 1795]

You tell me that my letters torture you; I will not describe
the effect yours have on me. . . . Certainly you are right;
our minds are not congenial. I have lived in an ideal
world, and fostered sentiments that you do not comprehend—or you would not treat me thus. . . . Be free— I
will not torment, when I cannot please. I can take care of
my child; you need not continually tell me that our fortune
is inseparable, *that you will try to cherish tenderness* for
me. Do no violence to yourself! . . . I want not protection
without affection; and support I need not, whilst my
faculties are undisturbed. . . . Adieu! I am agitated—my
whole frame is convulsed—my lips tremble, as if shook by
cold, though fire seems to be circulating in my veins.
[Sweden, August 1795]

To the fiat of fate I submit:—I am content to be wretched;
but I will not be contemptible.—Of me you have no cause
to complain, but for having had too much regard for

you—for having expected a degree of permanent happiness, when you only sought for a momentary gratification. [Hamburg, September 1795]

I write you now on my knees; imploring you to send my child and the maid . . . to Paris . . . When you receive this, my burning head will be cold. . . . I go to find comfort, and my only fear is that my poor body will be insulted by an endeavour to recall my hated existence. But I shall plunge into the Thames where there is the least chance of my being snatched from the death I seek. God bless you! May you never know by experience what you have made me endure. Should your sensibility ever awake, remorse will find its way to your heart; and, in the midst of business and sensual pleasure, I shall appear before you, the victim of your deviation from rectitude. [London, October 1795]

I have only to lament that, when the bitterness of death was past, I was inhumanly brought back to life and misery. But a fixed determination is not to be baffled by disappointment; nor will I allow that to be a frantic attempt, which was one of the calmest acts of reason. In this respect, I am only accountable to myself. . . . Your continually asserting, that you will do all in your power to contribute to my comfort (when you only allude to pecuniary assistance), appears to me a flagrant breach of delicacy.— I want not such vulgar comfort, nor will I accept it. I never wanted but your heart—that gone, you have nothing more to give. . . . When I am dead, respect for yourself will make you take care of the child. [London, November 1795]

My affection for you is rooted in my heart.— I know you are not what you now seem—nor will you always act, or feel, as you now do, though I may never be comforted by the change. . . . I have loved you with my whole soul, only to discover that I had no chance of a return . . . You seem to me only to have been anxious to shake me off —regardless whether you dashed me to atoms by the fall. [London, November 1795]

Resentment, and even anger, are momentary emotions with me—and I wished to tell you so, that if you ever think of me, it may not be in the light of an enemy. [London, December 1795]

As the parting from you for ever is the most serious event of my life, I will once more expostulate with you . . . . You urge "that your conduct was unequivocal."— It was not.— When your coolness has hurt me, with what tenderness have you endeavoured to remove the impression!— and even before I returned to England you took great pains to convince me that all my uneasiness was occasioned by the effect of a worn-out constitution—and you concluded your letter with these words, "Business alone has kept me from you.—Come to any port, and I will fly down to my two dear girls with a heart all their own." With these assurances, is it extraordinary that I should believe what I wished? . . . for God's sake, keep me no longer in suspense!— Let me see you once more! [London, December 1795]

You must do as you please with respect to the child.— I could wish that it might be done soon, that my name may be no more mentioned to you. It is now finished. . . . I now solemnly assure you, that this is an eternal farewell. . . . It is strange that, in spite of all you do, something like conviction forces me to believe that you are not what you appear to be. I part with you in peace. [London, December-March 1795-6]

I never blamed the woman for whom I was abandoned. I offered to see, nay, even to live with her, and I should have tried to improve her. But even she was deceived with respect to my character, and had her scruples when she heard the truth. [Letter to Godwin: London, July 1797]

It is far better to be often deceived than never to trust; to be disappointed in love than never to love; to lose a husband's fondness than forfeit his esteem. [*Rights of Woman*, 1792]

Godwin

William Godwin took his place as one of the intellectual giants of his day with the publication in 1793 of AN ENQUIRY CONCERNING POLITICAL JUSTICE, AND ITS INFLUENCE ON GENERAL VIRTUE AND HAPPINESS, in which he built a somewhat utopian case *for* the perfectibility of man and *against* institutions like private property, marriage, and organized religion. His exploration of the individual vis-à-vis society created a firestorm of public opinion.

When he and Mary first met, after the appearance of her equally provocative VINDICATION but before she left for France, he had found her abrasive. But after she returned to live in London in January 1796, he was captivated by her LETTERS FROM SWEDEN. By April, the "partiality" they conceived for one another "grew with equal advances in the mind of each," as he was to describe it in his 1798 MEMOIRS.

They lived in lodgings a few blocks apart, and retained this arrangement—since each believed in what we now call "space"—even after their friendship "melted" into love, Mary became pregnant, and they were quietly married at the end of March, 1797.

In the more or less daily exchange of notes that were carried back and forth by the maid, or delivered personally to each other's door, Mary gave free rein to her wit and gaiety, though her insecurity and petulance often came through as well.

Tragically, "this extraordinary pair," as they were called by a contemporary, was doomed. On August 30, Mary gave birth to a daughter, named Mary, rather than the "William" they had anticipated. On September 10, she died of the infection incurred when a doctor crudely removed the placenta, which had not made its appearance in the normal time.

I send you the last volume of "Héloïse" . . . and I want besides to remind you, when you write to me *verse*, not to choose the easiest task, my perfections, but to dwell on your own feelings—that is to say, give me a bird's-eye view of your heart. . . . I have observed that you compliment without rhyme or reason, when you are almost at a loss what to say. [July 1, 1796]

Had you called upon me yesterday I should have thanked you for your letter—and—perhaps, have told you that the sentence I *liked* best was the concluding one, where you tell me, that you were coming home, to depart *no more*— But now I am out of humour I mean to bottle up my kindness, unless something in your countenance, when I do see you, should make the cork fly out—whether I will or not. [July 21, 1796]

I called on you yesterday, in my way to dinner, not for Mary [the novel]—but to *bring* Mary— Is it necessary to tell your sapient Philosophership that I mean MYSELF. [August 11, 1796]

I have not lately passed so painful a night . . . My imagination is for ever betraying me into fresh misery, and I perceive that I shall be a child to the end of the chapter. . . . I would not be unjust for the world—I can only say that you appear to me to have acted injudiciously; and that full of your own feelings, little as I comprehend them, you forgot mine—or do not understand my character. [August 17, 1796]

I like your last—may I call it *love* letter? better than the first—and can I give you a higher proof of my esteem than to tell you . . . that it has calmed my mind—a mind that had been painfully active all the morning, haunted by old sorrows that seemed to come forward with new force to sharpen the present anguish. . . . You say you want soothing—will it sooth you to tell you the truth? I cannot hate you—I do not think you deserve it. Nay, more, I cannot withhold my friendship from you, and will try to merit yours, that *necessity* may bind you to me. . . . Now will you not be a good boy, and smile upon me . . . you ought to come and give me an appetite for my dinner, as you deprived me of one for my breakfast. [August 17, 1796]

I am never so well pleased with myself, as when I please you— I am not sure that please is the exact word to explain my sentiments—May I trust you to search in your own heart for the proper one? [August 27, 1796]

You are a tender considerate creature; but, entre nous, do not make too many philosophical experiments, for when a philosopher is put on his metal, to use your own phrase, there is no knowing where he will stop—and I have not reckoned on having a wild-goose chase after a—wise man. [September 10, 1796]

Now by these presents let me assure you that you are not only in my heart, but my veins, this morning. I turn from you half abashed—yet you haunt me, and some look, word or touch thrills through my whole frame—yes, at the very moment when I am labouring to think of something, if not somebody, else. Get ye gone Intruder! though I am forced to add dear . . . When the heart and reason accord there is no flying from voluptuous sensations, I find, do what a woman can—Can a philosopher do more? [September 13, 1796]

. . . this is not, I believe, a day sufficiently to be depended on, to tempt us to set out in search of rural felicity. We must then woo philosophy *chez vous* ce soir, n'est-ce pas; for I do not like to lose my Philosopher even in the lover. [September 15, 1796]

You once talked of giving me one of your keys, I then could admit myself without tying you down to an hour, which I cannot always punctually observe in the character of a woman, unless I tacked that of a wife to it. . . . I am glad that you force me to love you more and more, in spite of my fear of being pierced to the heart by every one on whom I rest my mighty stock of affection. [September 30, 1796]

I should have liked to have dined with you to day, after finishing your essay . . . this morning—reminding myself, every now and then, that the writer *loved me*. . . . It is not rapture.— It is a sublime tranquillity. I have felt it in your arms . . . I wish I may find you at home when I carry this letter to drop it in the box,—that I may drop a kiss with it into your heart, to be embalmed, till we meet. [October 4, 1796]

I send you your household linen— I am not sure that I did not feel a sensation of pleasure at thus acting the part of a wife, though you have so little respect for the character. There is such a magic in affection that I have been more gratified by your clasping your hands round my arm, in company, than I could have been by all the admiration in the world. [November 10, 1796]

I have seldom seen so much live fire running about my features as this morning when recollections—very dear, called forth the blush of pleasure, as I adjusted my hair. [November 13, 1796]

I wish you would always take my ye for a ye; and my nay for a nay. It torments me to be obliged to guess at, or guard against, false interpretations—and, while I am wishing, I will add another—that you would distinguish between jest and earnest, to express myself elegantly. To give you a criterion. I never play with edged-tools . . . for when I am really hurt or angry I am dreadfully serious. Still, allow me a little more tether than is necessary . . . Let me, I pray thee! have a sort of *comparative* freedom, as you are a profound Grammarian, to run round, as good, better, best;—cheerful, gay, playful; nay even frolicksome, once a year. [November 19, 1796]

You tell me that "I spoil little attentions, by anticipation." Yet to have attention, I find that it is necessary to demand it. . . . I *did* expect you last night— But, *never mind it.* Your coming would not have been worth any thing, if it must be requested. [November 28, 1796]

I am not well, to day, yet I scarcely know what to complain of, excepting extreme lowness of spirits. I felt it creeping over me last night; but I will strive against it instead of talking of it— I hate this torpor of mind and senses. [December 6, 1796]

There was a tenderness in your manner, as you seemed to be opening your heart to a new born affection that rendered you very dear to me. There are other pleasures in the world, you perceive, beside those known to your philosophy. [December 23, 1796]

I believe I ought to beg your pardon for talking at you, last night, though it was in sheer simplicity of heart—and I have been asking myself why it so happen— Faith and troth it is because there was nobody else worth attacking, or who could converse . . . be assured, when I find a man that has any thing in him, I shall let my every day dish alone. [January 13, 1797]

Still have the inelegant complaint, which no novelist has yet ventured to mention as one of the consequences of sentimental distress. [January 24, 1797]

Pray send me . . . for my luncheon, a part of the supper you announced to me last night—as I am to be a partaker of your worldly goods—you know! [March 31, 1797]

. . . when I press any thing it is always with a true *wifish* submission to your judgment and inclination. [April 8, 1797]

I am well and tranquil, excepting the disturbance produced by Master William's joy, who took it into his head to frisk a little at being informed of your remembrance. I begin to love this little creature, and to anticipate his birth as a fresh twist to a knot, which I do not wish to untie. . . . I love you better than I supposed I did, when I promised to love you for ever—and I will add what will gratify your benevolence, if not your heart, that on the whole I may be termed happy. You are a tender, affectionate creature; and I feel it thrilling through my frame, giving and promising pleasure. [June 6, 1797]

William is all alive—and my appearance no longer doubtful—you, I dare say, will perceive the difference. What a fine thing it is to be a man! [June 10, 1797]

. . . you have been a week on the road . . . I am at a loss to guess how you could have been from saturday to sunday night traveling from C[oventry] to C[ambridge]— In short—your being so late to night, and the chance of your not coming, shews so little consideration, that unless you suppose me to be a stick or a stone, you must have forgot to think—as well as to feel, since you have been on the wing. I am afraid to add what I feel— Good night. [June 19, 1797]

To be frank with you, your behaviour yesterday brought on my troublesome pain. But I lay no great stress on that circumstance, because, were not my health in a more delicate state than usual, it could not be so easily affected. I am absurd to look for the affection which I have only found in my own tormented heart; and how can you blame me for taken refuge in the idea of a God, when I despair of finding sincerity on earth? . . . You judge not in your own case as in that of another. You give a softer name to folly and immorality when it flatters . . . your vanity. [July 4, 1797]

I have no doubt of seeing the animal to day; but must wait for Mrs Blenkinsop [a midwife] to guess at the hour— I have sent for her— Pray send me the news paper— I wish I had a novel, or some book of sheer amusement, to excite curiosity, and while away the time— Have you anything of the kind? [August 30, 1797]

Mrs Blenkinsop tells me that Every thing is in a fair way, and that there is no fear of the event being put off till another day— Still, *at present*, she thinks, I shall not immediately be freed from my load—I am very well— Call before dinner time, unless you receive another message from me. [August 30, 1797]

Mrs Blenkinsop tells me that I am in the most natural state, and can promise me a safe delivery—But that I must have a little patience [August 30, 1797]

"Author"

Wollstonecraft wrote very little about writing per se. But she was very proud of being "an author," as seen in the few references she makes in letters to family and friends. And when she became famous, she was happy to advise others.

Actually, her own writing—particularly in the two VINDICATIONS—was often far from perfect, and much of it is very hard to plough through today. Many sentences, paragraphs, and even whole chapters, are virtually unreadable because of their complex structure or their repetitiousness. In the fever of excitement that possessed her as her ideas poured out, she wrote too quickly and carelessly, and didn't take the time to go back and hone the material.

Her "fictions" are even more difficult for the modern reader—she was not a Jane Austen (although one would like to imagine that Austen, who was seventeen when VINDICATION appeared, was influenced by the independent woman Wollstonecraft envisioned).

. . . if I make any conquests in Ireland it will be owing to the *blue hat*—which is the first phenomenon of the kind, that has made its appearance in this hemisphere— There is a period for you!—worthy of an author whose work [THOUGHTS ON THE EDUCATION OF DAUGHTERS] is just ushered into the world. [Letter to Everina: Mitchelstown, January 1787]

My nerves daily grow worse and worse—yet I strive to occupy my mind even when duty does not force me to do it . . . when I have more strength I read Philosophy—and write— I *hope* you have not forgot that I am an Author. [Letter to Eliza: Bristol, June 1787]

Spite of my vexations, I have lately written a fiction which I intend to give to the world [MARY, A FICTION]; it is a tale, to illustrate an opinion of mine, that a genius will educate itself. [Letter to Reverend Gabell: Henley, September 1787]

Mr Johnson . . . assures me that if I exert my talents in writing I may support myself in a comfortable way. I am then going to be the first of a new genus—I tremble at the attempt. [Letter to Everina: London, November 1787]

I have given him MARY—and . . . shall finish another book for young people [ORIGINAL STORIES FROM REAL LIFE], which I think has some merit. [Letter to Everina: London, November 1787]

Though your remarks are generally judicious—I cannot *now* concur with you, I mean with respect to the preface [of ORIGINAL STORIES], and have not altered it. I hate the usual smooth way of exhibiting proud humility. A general rule *only* extends to the majority—and, believe me, the few judicious parents who may peruse my book, will not feel themselves hurt—and the weak are too vain to mind what is said in a book intended for children. [Letter to Joseph Johnson: London, 1787-8]

It is not necessary, with courtly insincerity . . . to profess that I think it an honour to discuss an important subject with a man whose literary abilities have raised him to notice in the state. I have not yet learned to twist my periods, nor, in the equivocal idiom of politeness, to disguise my sentiments, and imply what I should be afraid to utter: if, therefore, in the course of this epistle, I chance to express contempt, and even indignation, with some emphasis, I beseech you to believe that it is not a flight of fancy; for truth . . . has ever appeared to me the essence of the sublime . . . I do not condescend to cull my words to avoid the invidious phrase. [*Rights of Men*, 1790]

I am actually sitting for the picture. . . . I do not imagine that it will be a very striking likeness; but, if you do not find me in it, I will send you a more faithful sketch—a book [A VINDICATION OF THE RIGHTS OF WOMAN] that I am now writing, in which *I* myself . . . shall certainly appear, head and heart. [Letter to William Roscoe: London, October 1791]

I shall give the last sheet to the printer to day; and, I am dissatisfied with myself for not having done justice to the subject.—Do not suspect me of false modesty—I mean to say, that had I allowed myself more time I could have written a better book, in every sense of the word. . . . I intend to finish the next volume before I begin to print, for it is not pleasant to have the [printer's] Devil coming for the conclusion of a sheet before it is written. [Letter to William Roscoe: London, January 1792]

I aim at being useful, and sincerity will render me unaffected; for, wishing rather to persuade by the force of my arguments, than dazzle by the elegance of my language, I shall not waste my time in rounding periods, or in fabricating the turgid bombast of artificial feelings, which, coming from the head, never reach the heart.—I shall be employed about things, not words!—and, anxious to render my sex more respectable members of society, I shall try to avoid that flowery diction which has slided from essays into novels, and from novels into familiar letters and conversation. [*Rights of Woman*, 1792]

. . . my book has been translated [into French] and praised in some popular prints. [Letter to Everina: London, June 1792]

I do not approve of your preface . . . Disadvantages of education &c ought, in my opinion, never to be pleaded (with the public) in excuse for defects of any importance, because if the writer has not sufficient strength of mind to overcome the common difficulties which lie in his way, nature seems to command him, with a very audible voice, to leave the task of instructing others to those who can. This kind of vain humility has ever disgusted me—and I should say to an author, who humbly sued for forbearance, "if you have not a tolerably good opinion of your own production, why intrude it on the public? we have plenty of bad books already, that have just gasped for breath and died.". . . An author, especially a woman, should be cautious lest she too hastily swallows the crude praises which partial friend and polite acquaintance bestow thoughtlessly when the supplicating eye looks for them. In short, it requires great resolution to try rather to be useful than to please. . . . Rest on yourself—if your essays have merit they will stand alone, if not the *shouldering up* of Dr this or that will not long keep them from falling to the ground. . . . Indeed the preface . . . is too full of your-self. . . till a work strongly interests the public, true modesty should keep the author in the back ground—for it is only about the character and life of a *good* author that anxiety is active. [Letter to Mary Hays: London, November 1792]

I am now at the house of an old Gardener writing a great book [AN HISTORICAL AND MORAL VIEW . . . OF THE FRENCH REVOLUTION]; and in better health and spirits than I have ever enjoyed since I came to France. [Letter to Eliza: Neuilly-sur-Seine, June 1793]

I have begun [LETTERS WRITTEN DURING A SHORT RESIDENCE IN SWEDEN, NORWAY, AND DENMARK], which will, I hope, discharge all my obligations of a pecuniary kind.— I am lowered in my own eyes, on account of my not having done it sooner. [Letter to Imlay: Norway, July 1795]

In writing these desultory letters, I found I could not avoid being continually the first person . . . I tried to correct this fault, if it be one, for they were designed for publica-tion; but in proportion as I arranged my thoughts, my letter, I found, became stiff and affected: I therefore determined to let my remarks and reflections flow unre-strained. . . . avoiding those details which . . . appear very insipid to those who only accompany you in their chair. [*Short Residence*, 1795]

. . . you remarked, relative to my manner of writing—that there was a radical defect in it . . . What is to be done, I must either disregard your opinion, think it unjust, or throw down my pen in despair. . . . I must reckon on doing some good, and getting the money I want, by my writings, or go to sleep for ever. . . . I am compelled to think that there is some thing in my writings more valuable than in the productions of some people on whom you bestow warm elogiums— I mean more mind—denominate it as you will—more of the observations of my own senses, more of the combining of my own imagination—the effusions of my own feelings and passions than the cold workings of the brain on the materials procured by the senses and imagination of other writers. [Letter to Godwin: London, September 1796]

. . . now you have led me to discover that I write worse than I thought I did, there is no stopping short— I must improve, or be dissatisfied with myself. [Letter to Godwin: London, September 1796]

I am vexed and surprised at your not thinking the situation of Maria [heroine of THE WRONGS OF WOMAN] sufficiently important, and can only account for this want of—shall I say it?—delicacy of feeling by recollecting that you are a man. [Letter to George Dyson: London, May 1797]

Part Two

OPINIONS
AND OBSERVATIONS

With the strengthened confidence in her abilities
that followed the success of A VINDICATION OF THE
RIGHTS OF MEN (her reply to Burke on the French
Revolution) in 1790, Wollstonecraft went on almost immediately to produce A VINDICATION OF
THE RIGHTS OF WOMAN. "Never," wrote Godwin,
"did any author enter into a cause, with a more
ardent desire to be . . . an effectual champion."
She wrote the book, at fever pitch, in six weeks.

A hundred years later, in the first major up-
surge of interest in Wollstonecraft since her death,
Elizabeth Robins Pennell's biography of her was
included in a British publisher's Eminent Women
Series. "She must always be honoured," Pennell
concluded, "for her integrity of motive, her fear-
lessness of action, and her faithful devotion to the
cause of humanity."

In 1992, in commemoration of the 200th anni-
versary of VINDICATION, Virginia Sapiro—a pro-
fessor of both political science and women's
studies at the University of Wisconsin—published

A Vindication of Political Virtue. Her object is to show that *all* of Wollstonecraft's writings were consistent with a unified political theory.

THE INDIVIDUAL

"She offered," writes Sapiro, "a means of stretching the liberal temperament to incorporate into political thinking explicit concern for the quality of the personal relations and day-to-day conditions of the lives of citizens." But while Wollstonecraft considered reason, religion, and moral values essential to the improvement of both individual and society, she also took into account the senses, the passions, and the imagination.

SOCIETY

When she took on the social institutions that oppress humanity under tyranny, and women in a male-dominated society, Wollstonecraft's passion for social justice ranged over a broad spectrum. Permeating all her writings are a number of interlocking themes, among them the subjugation of women by marriage and the necessity of education for girls; the evils of inherited property and the degradation of the working poor; the venality of British politics and the ideals epitomized by the French Revolution.

THE INDIVIDUAL

Life

Wollstonecraft was very early disillusioned with
life, yet her belief in God and the blessings to
come in the next world sustained her, as did her
hunger for knowledge and the need to share it.

Young people generally set out with romantic and sanguine hopes of happiness, and must receive a great many
stings before they are convinced of their mistake, and that
they are pursuing a mere phantom, an empty name. [Letter
to Jane Arden: Bath, ca May-June 1779]

Reason, as well as religion, convinces me all has happen'd
for the best. This is an old worn-out maxim; but 'tis not
the less true—for I am persuaded misfortunes are of the
greatest service, as they set things in the light they ought
to be view'd in; and give those that are tried by them, a
kind of early old age. . . . The keen blast of adversity has
not frozen my heart—so far from it that I cannot be quite
miserable while one of my fellow-creatures enjoys some
portion of content. [Letter to Jane Arden: Bath, October 1779]

I don't know which is the worst—to think too little or too much.—'tis a difficult matter to draw the line, and keep clear of melancholy and thoughtlessness:—I really think it is best sometimes to be deceived—and to expect what we are never likely to meet with;—deluded by false hopes, the time would seem shorter, while we are hastening to a better world where the follies and weaknesses that disturb us in this will be no more. [Letter to Jane Arden: Windsor, ca April-June, 1780]

Do try . . . to encourage hope—without this pleasing delusion life is dull indeed—and no undertaking is carried on with vigour. [Letter to George Blood: Newington Green, July 1785]

Life glides away—and we should be careful not to let it pass without leaving some useful traces behind it. [Letter to Eliza: Newington Green, September 1786]

. . . our whole life is but an education for eternity. [Letter to Everina: Dublin, February 1787]

. . . life loses its zest when we find that there is nothing worth wishing for, nothing to detain the thoughts in the present scene but what quickly grows stale, rendering the soul torpid or uneasy. [Letter to Everina: London, September 1792]

Life is but a labour of patience: it is always rolling a great stone up a hill; for, before a person can find a resting-place, imagining it is lodged, down it comes again, and all the work is to be done over anew! . . . The world appears an "unweeded garden" where "things rank and vile" flourish best. [Letter to Imlay: Paris, January 1794]

Reaching the cascade . . . my soul was hurried . . . into a new train of reflections. The impetuous dashing of the rebounding torrent from the dark cavities which mocked the exploring eye produced an equal activity in my mind: my thoughts darted from earth to heaven, and I asked myself why I was chained to life and its misery? Still, the tumultuous emotions this sublime object excited were pleasurable; and, viewing it, my soul rose, with renewed dignity, above its cares—grasping at immortality. [*Short Residence*, 1795]

I viewed, with a mixture of pity and horrour, these beings [soldiers] training to be sold to slaughter, or be slaughtered, and fell into reflections on an old opinion of mine, that it is the preservation of the species, not of individuals, which appears to be the design of the Deity throughout the whole of nature. Blossoms come forth only to be blighted; fish lay their spawn where it will be devoured; and what a large portion of the human race are born merely to be swept prematurely away. Does not this waste of budding life emphatically assert, that it is not men, but man, whose preservation is so necessary to the completion of the grand plan of the universe? [*Short Residence*, 1795]

. . . it is wisdom, I believe, to extract as much happiness as we can out of the various ills of life—for who has not cause to be miserable, if they will allow themselves to think so? [Letter to Mary Hays: London, 1796]

Values

Virtue, principle, sincerity, and morality were Wollstonecraft's guideposts to the life worth living, while prejudice, hypocrisy, dishonesty, and the pursuit of false goals were her *bêtes noires*. Variations on these themes occur throughout her letters and published work.

. . . suffer not the seeds of virtue in your bosom to lie dormant or to be choked by a mistaken fondness for present gratifications. [Letter to George Blood: London, January 1788]

. . . without fixed principles, even goodness of heart is no security from inconsistency, and mild affectionate sensibility only renders a man more ingeniously cruel, when the pangs of hurt vanity are mistaken for virtuous indignation, and the gall of bitterness for the milk of Christian charity. [*Rights of Men*, 1790]

. . . it is a farce to call any being virtuous whose virtues do not result from the exercise of its own reason. [*Rights of Woman*, 1792]

. . . it is not possible to give a young person a just view of life; he must have struggled with his own passions before he can estimate the force of the temptation which betrayed his brother into vice . . . The world cannot be seen by an unmoved spectator, we must mix in the throng, and feel as men feel before we can judge of their feelings. If we mean, in short, to live in the world to grow wiser and better, and not merely to enjoy the good things of life, we must attain a knowledge of others at the same time that we become acquainted with ourselves—knowledge acquired any other way only hardens the heart and perplexes the understanding. [*Rights of Woman*, 1792]

Most prospects in life are marred by the shuffling worldly wisdom of men who, forgetting that they cannot serve God and mammon, endeavour to blend contradictory things.—If you wish to make your son rich, pursue one course—if you are only anxious to make him virtuous, you must take another; but do not imagine that you can bound from one road to the other without losing your way. [*Rights of Woman*, 1792]

. . . with respect to reputation, the attention is confined to a single virtue—chastity. If the honour of a woman, as it is absurdly called, be safe, she may neglect every social duty, nay, ruin her family by gaming and extravagance, yet still present a shameless front—for truly she is an honourable woman! [*Rights of Woman*, 1792]

Few, I believe, have had much affection for mankind, who did not first love their parents, their brothers, sisters, and even the domestic brutes whom they first played with. The exercise of youthful sympathies forms the moral temperature. [*Rights of Woman*, 1792]

Be not too anxious to get money!—for nothing worth having is to be purchased. [Letter to Imlay: Paris, December 1793]

We must get entirely clear of all the notions drawn from the wild traditions of original sin . . . on which priests have erected their tremendous structures of imposition to persuade us that we are naturally inclined to evil; we shall then leave room for the expansion of the human heart, and, I trust, find that men will insensibly render each other happier as they grow wiser. [*Revolution*, 1794]

. . . the house smelt of commerce from top to toe—so that his abortive attempt to display taste only proved it to be one of the things not to be bought with gold. [Letter to Imlay: Havre, August 1794]

. . . he has the idle desire to amass a large fortune . . . merely to have the credit of having made it. But we who are governed by other motives ought not to be led on by him. . . . it will be better, in future, to pursue some sober plan, which may demand more time, and still enable you to arrive at the same end. It appears to me absurd to waste life in preparing to live. [Letter to Imlay: Paris, December 1794]

How much of the virtue which appears in the world is put on for the world! And how little dictated by self respect. [*Short Residence*, 1795]

To be honester than the laws require is by most people thought a work of supererogation; and to slip through the grate of the law has ever exercised the abilities of adventurers who wish to get rich the shortest way. Knavery, without personal danger, is an art brought to great perfection by the statesman and swindler; and meaner knaves are not tardy in following their footsteps. [*Short Residence*, 1795]

. . . under whatever point of view I consider society, it appears to me that an adoration of property is the root of all evil. [*Short Residence*, 1795]

Lutherans, preaching reformation, have built a reputation for sanctity on the same foundation as the catholics; yet I do not perceive that a regular attendance on public worship, and their other observances, make them a whit more true in their affections or honest in their private transactions. It seems, indeed, quite as easy to prevaricate with religious injunctions as human laws. [*Short Residence*, 1795]

Men are strange machines, and their whole system of morality is in general held together by one grand principle, which loses its force the moment they allow themselves to break with impunity over the bounds which secured their self-respect. A man ceases to love humanity, and then individuals, as he advances in the chase after wealth, as one clashes with his interest, the other with his pleasures; to business, as it is termed, every thing must give way, nay, is sacrificed, and all the endearing charities of citizen, husband, father, brother, become empty names. [*Short Residence*, 1795]

Reason and Prejudice

Wollstonecraft had no patience with people whose lives were ruled by irrational opinions, and many of her strictures on education are aimed at teaching individuals to draw their own conclusions from facts and personal experience.

. . . to attempt to lead or govern a weak mind is impossible; it will ever press forward to what it wishes regardless of impediments and with a selfish eagerness to believe what it desires practicable tho' the contrary is as clear as the noon day. . . . May my habitation never be fixed among the tribe that can't look beyond the present gratification—that draw fixed conclusions from general rules—that attend to the literal meaning only—and because a thing ought to be expect that it will come to pass. [Letter to Everina: Bermondsey, January 1784]

The pictures that the imagination draws are so very delightful that we willing let it predominate over reason till experience forces us to see the truth . . . and tho' we declare in general terms that there is no such thing as happiness on Earth yet it requires severe disappointments to make us forbear to seek it and be contented with endeavoring to prepare for a better state. [Letter to Everina: ?Hackney, January 1784]

Quitting now the flowers of rhetoric, let us, Sir, reason together; and, believe me, I should not have meddled with these troubled waters, in order to point out your inconsistencies, if your wit had not burnished up some rusty baneful opinions, and swelled the shallow current of ridicule till it resembled the flow of reason, and presumed to be the test of truth. . . . I glow with indignation when I attempt, methodically, to unravel your slavish paradoxes, in which I can find no fixed first principles to refute; I shall not, therefore, condescend to shew where you affirm in one page what you deny in another; and how frequently you draw conclusions without any previous premises:—it would be something like cowardice to fight with a man who had never exercised the weapons which his opponent chose to combat with. [*Rights of Men*, 1790]

. . . I respect an opponent, though he tenaciously maintains opinions in which I cannot coincide; but, if I once discover that many of those opinions are empty rhetorical flourishes, the respect is soon changed into that pity which borders on contempt; and the mock dignity and haughty stalk, only reminds me of the ass in the lion's skin. [*Rights of Men*, 1790]

When we read a book that supports our favourite opinions, how eagerly do we suck in the doctrines, and suffer our minds placidly to reflect the images that illustrate the tenets we have embraced. We indolently acquiesce in the conclusion, and our spirit animates and corrects the various subjects. But when . . . we peruse a skilful writer with whom we do not coincide in opinion, how attentive is the mind to detect fallacy. [*Rights of Men*, 1790]

Men, in general, seem to employ their reason to justify prejudices, which they have imbibed, they can scarcely trace how, rather than to root them out. The mind must be strong that resolutely forms its own principles; for a kind of intellectual cowardice prevails which makes many men shrink from the task, or only do it by halves. [*Rights of Woman*, 1792]

. . . what a weak barrier is truth when it stands in the way of an hypothesis! [*Rights of Woman*, 1792]

When, in a circle of strangers, or acquaintances, a person of moderate abilities asserts an opinion with heat, I will venture to affirm . . . that it is a prejudice. These echoes have a high respect for the understanding of some relation or friend, and without fully comprehending the opinions which they are so eager to retail, they maintain them with a degree of obstinacy that would surprise even the person who concocted them. [*Rights of Woman*, 1792]

. . . moss-covered opinions assume the disproportioned form of prejudices, when they are indolently adopted only because age has given them a venerable aspect, though the reason on which they were built ceases to be a reason, or cannot be traced. . . . A prejudice is a fond obstinate persuasion for which we can give no reason; for the moment a reason can be given for an opinion, it ceases to be a prejudice, though it may be an error in judgment. [*Rights of Woman*, 1792]

. . . it generally happens that people assert their opinions with the greatest heat when they begin to waver; striving to drive out their own doubts by convincing their opponent, they grow angry when those gnawing doubts are thrown back to prey on themselves. [*Rights of Woman*, 1792]

The greater number of people take their opinions on trust to avoid the trouble of exercising their own minds, and these indolent beings naturally adhere to the letter, rather than the spirit, of a law, divine or human. [*Rights of Woman*, 1792]

If the power of reflecting on the past, and darting the keen eye of contemplation into futurity, be the grand privilege of man, it must be granted that some people enjoy this prerogative in a very limited degree. Every thing new appears to them wrong; and not able to distinguish the possible from the monstrous, they fear where no fear should find a place, running from the light of reason, as if it were a firebrand. [*Rights of Woman*, 1792]

Prudence is ever the resort of weakness; and they rarely go as far as they may in any undertaking, who are determined not to go beyond it on any account. [*Short Residence*, 1795]

"Dress and Ridicule"

During the years Wollstonecraft worked as companion to a wealthy woman and as governess in an aristocratic family, she had ample opportunity to observe the superficial existence of the idle classes. This experience provided her with many of the specific examples of the wasted lives of women that she was to incorporate into her early books, as well as into VINDICATION.

GENTILITY

I am particularly sick of genteel life, as it is called;—the unmeaning civilities that I see every day practiced don't agree with my temper;—I long for a little sincerity, and look forward with pleasure to the time when I shall lay aside all restraint. [Letter to Jane Arden: Windsor, ca April-June 1780]

She . . . brings up her daughters in a stile I dont approve of—that is, she seems to wish rather to make them accomplished and fashionable than good and sensible, in the true sense of the word:—In this she follows the crowd, and it is much to be lamented that the Stream runs so rapidly that way. [Letter to Jane Arden: Windsor, June-August, 1780]

. . . [I] am afraid a school would not succeed (and this fear arises from experience) without I could take a house and set off in a genteel style— Poverty will oftener raise contempt than pity—and . . . to gain the respect of the vulgar (a term which I with propriety apply to the generality, however weighty their purses), you must dazzle their senses—and even not appear to want their assistance if you expect to have it . . . The drapery is what catches the superficial eye—and the necessary appendage, wealth, will go much farther than the most shining abilities to make a person respected— In Ireland I know they are particularly attentive to appearances, and the first impression is of the utmost consequence. [Letter to George Blood: Newington Green, July 1786]

I could not live the life they lead . . . nothing but dress and ridicule going forward—and I really believe their fondness for ridicule tends to make them affected—the women in their manners, and the men in their conversation—for witlings abound—and *puns* fly about like crackers, tho' you would scarcely guess they had any meaning in them, if you did not hear the noise they create. [Letter to Everina: Eton, October 1786]

. . . and as to the great world and its frivolous ceremonies. . . I thank Heaven that I was not so unfortunate as to be born a Lady of quality. [Letter to Everina: Dublin, March 1787]

I have been lost in stupidity, listening to the chat of some people of quality, and wished *even* for vulgar humor to have seasoned it. [Letter to Eliza: Bristol, June 1787]

APPEARANCE

It is true, regular features strike at first; but it is a well ordered mind which occasions those turns of expression in the countenance, which make a lasting impression. [*Education of Daughters*, Artificial Manners, 1787]

By far too much of a girl's time is taken up in dress. . . The body hides the mind, and it is, in its turn, obscured by the drapery. I hate to see the frame of a picture so glaring as to catch the eye and divide the attention. Dress ought to adorn the person, and not rival it. . . . The beauty of dress (I shall raise astonishment by saying so) is . . . when it neither distorts or hides the human form by unnatural protuberances. [*Education of Daughters*, Dress, 1787]

. . . the whole tribe of beauty-washes, cosmetics, Olympian dew, oriental herbs, liquid bloom . . . . are advertised in so ridiculous a style, that the rapid sale of them is a very severe reflection on the understanding of those females who encourage it. . . . and if, caught by it, a man marries a woman thus disguised, he may chance not to be satisfied with her real person. . . . nor does a woman's dressing herself in a way to attract languishing glances give us the most advantageous opinion of the purity of her mind. [*Education of Daughters*, Dress, 1787]

Men order their clothes to be made, and have done with the subject; women make their own clothes, necessary or ornamental, and are continually talking about them; and their thoughts follow their hands. It is not indeed the making of necessaries that weakens the mind, but the frippery of dress. [*Rights of Woman*, 1792]

The thoughts of women ever hover round their persons, and is it surprising that their persons are reckoned most valuable? . . . sedentary employments render the majority of women sickly—and false notions of female excellence make them proud of this delicacy, though it be another fetter, that by calling the attention continually to the body, cramps the activity of the mind. [*Rights of Woman*, 1792]

The air of fashion, which many young people are so eager to attain, always strikes me like the studied attitudes of some modern pictures, copied with tasteless servility after the antiques;—the soul is left out, and none of the parts are tied together by what may properly be termed character. This varnish of fashion . . . may dazzle the weak; but leave nature to itself, and it will seldom disgust the wise. [*Rights of Woman*, 1792]

BEHAVIOR

I hate formality and compliments; one affectionate word would give me more pleasure than all the pretty things that come from the head; but have nothing to say to the heart. [Letter to Eliza: Windsor, August 1780]

The lively thoughtlessness of youth makes every young creature agreeable for the time; but when those years are flown, and sense is not substituted in the stead of vivacity, the follies of youth are acted over, and they never consider that the things which please in their proper season disgust out of it. It is very absurd to see a woman, whose brow time has marked with wrinkles, aping the manners of a girl in her teens. [*Education of Daughters*, Exterior Accomplishments, 1787]

That gentleness of behaviour, which makes us courteous to all, and that benevolence, which makes us loth to offend any and studious to please every creature, is sometimes copied by the polite; but how aukward is the copy! The warmest professions of regard are prostituted on all occasions. . . . and the esteem which is only due to merit appears to be lavished on all . . . Civility is due to all, but regard or admiration should never be expressed when it is not felt. [*Education of Daughters*, Artificial Manners, 1787]

Let the manners arise from the mind, and let there be no disguise for the genuine emotions of the heart. [*Education of Daughters*, Artificial Manners, 1787]

True politeness is a polish, not a varnish; and should rather be acquired by observation than admonition. [*Original Stories*, Preface, 1788]

. . . complicated rules to adjust behaviour are a weak substitute for simple principles. [*Rights of Woman*, 1792]

It is time to effect a revolution in female manners—time to restore to them their lost dignity—and make them, as a part of the human species, labour by reforming themselves to reform the world. [*Rights of Woman*, 1792]

I lament that women are systematically degraded by receiving the trivial attentions which men think it manly to pay to the sex . . . So ludicrous, in fact, do these ceremonies appear to me, that I scarcely am able to govern my muscles, when I see a man start with eager and serious solicitude to lift a handkerchief, or shut a door, when the *lady* could have done it herself had she only moved a pace or two. [*Rights of Woman*, 1792]

Make the heart clean, and give the head employment, and I will venture to predict that there will be nothing offensive in the behaviour. [*Rights of Woman*, 1792]

. . . the reading of novels makes women, and particularly ladies of fashion, very fond of using strong expressions and superlatives in conversation; and, though the dissipated artificial life which they lead prevents their cherishing any strong legitimate passion, the language of passion in affected tones slips for ever from their glib tongues, and every trifle produces those phosphoric bursts which only mimick in the dark the flame of passion. [*Rights of Woman*, 1792]

Hospitality has, I think, been too much praised by travellers as a proof of goodness of heart, when in my opinion indiscriminate hospitality is rather a criterion by which you may form a tolerable estimate of the indolence or vacancy of a head, or, in other words, a fondness for social pleasures in which the mind not having its proportion of exercise, the bottle must be pushed about. [*Short Residence*, 1795]

SOCIETY

Men/Women

Before she became a "champion," Wollstonecraft could write quite lightheartedly about her views on the battle of the sexes. Even in the context of her more serious, and often ponderous, VINDICATION, flashes of humor seem to come through in spite of herself.

. . . the Prince of Wales is the principal beau here;—all the damsels set their caps at him, and . . . the poor girls he condescends to take notice of are pulled to pieces:—the withered old maids sagaciously hint their fears, and kindly remark that they always thought them forward things: you would suppose a smile or a look of his had something fatal in it, and that a maid could not look at him and remain pure. [Letter to Jane Arden: Windsor, June-August 1780]

. . . the men [in Ireland] are dreadful flirts, so take care of your heart, and don't leave it in the Bogs.—Preserve your cheerful temper, and laugh & dance when a fiddle comes in your way, but beware of the sly collectors; . . . You are a good girl—I would therefore have you grow fat, and your good nature and obliging temper will always ensure you admirers that will have sense enough to prefer such good qualities to a baby face:—For my part—I have already got the wrinkles of old age, and so, like a true woman, rail at what I don't possess. [Letter to Jane Arden: Walham Green, ca 1782-83]

Let there be . . . no coercion *established* in society, and the common law of gravity prevailing, the sexes will fall into their proper places. And, now that more equitable laws are forming your citizens . . . I wish . . . to set some investigations of this kind afloat in France; and should they lead to a confirmation of my principles, when your constitution is revised the Rights of Woman may be respected, if it be fully proved that reason calls for this respect, and loudly demands JUSTICE for one half of the human race. [*Rights of Woman*, 1792]

. . . the civilized women of the present century, with a few exceptions, are only anxious to inspire love, when they ought to cherish a nobler ambition, and by their abilities and virtues exact respect. [*Rights of Woman*, 1792]

In the government of the physical world it is observable that the female in point of strength is, in general, inferior to the male. This is the law of nature; and it does not appear to be suspended or abrogated in favour of woman. A degree of physical superiority cannot, therefore, be denied—and it is a noble prerogative! But not content with this natural preeminence, men endeavor to sink us still lower, merely to render us alluring objects for a moment; and women, intoxicated by the adoration which men, under the influence of their senses, pay them, do not seek to obtain a durable interest in their hearts, or to become the friends of the fellow creatures who find amusement in their society. [*Rights of Woman*, 1792]

My own sex, I hope, will excuse me, if I treat them like rational creatures, instead of . . . viewing them as if they were in a state of perpetual childhood, unable to stand alone. [*Rights of Woman*, 1792]

I wish to shew that elegance is inferior to virtue, that the first object of laudable ambition is to obtain a character as a human being, regardless of the distinction of sex. [*Rights of Woman*, 1792]

Women are told from their infancy, and taught by the example of their mothers, that a little knowledge of human weakness, justly termed cunning, softness of temper, *outward* obedience, and a scrupulous attention to a puerile kind of propriety, will obtain for them the protection of man; and should they be beautiful, every thing else is needless, for, at least, twenty years of their lives. [*Rights of Woman*, 1792]

. . . idleness has produced a mixture of gallantry and despotism into society, which leads the very men who are the slaves of their mistresses to tyrannize over their sisters, wives, and daughters. . . . Strengthen the female mind by enlarging it, and there will be an end to blind obedience; but, as blind obedience is ever sought for by power, tyrants and sensualists are in the right when they endeavour to keep women in the dark, because the former only want slaves, and the latter a play-thing. The sensualist, indeed, has been the most dangerous of tyrants, and women have been duped by their lovers, as princes by their ministers, whilst dreaming that they reigned over them. [*Rights of Woman*, 1792]

[Rousseau] insinuates that truth and fortitude, the corner stones of all human virtue, should be cultivated with certain restrictions, because, with respect to the female character, obedience is the grand lesson which ought to be impressed with unrelenting rigour. What nonsense! when will a great man arise with sufficient strength of mind to puff away the fumes which pride and sensuality have thus spread over the subject! [*Rights of Woman*, 1792]

To endeavor to reason love out of the world, would be to out-Quixote Cervantes, and equally offend against common sense; but an endeavour . . . to prove that it should not be allowed to dethrone superior powers . . . appears less wild. [*Rights of Woman*, 1792]

Love, the common passion, in which chance and sensation take place of choice and reason, is in some degree, felt by the mass of mankind . . . This passion, naturally increased by suspense and difficulties, draws the mind out of its accustomed state, and exalts the affections. [*Rights of Woman*, 1792]

Gentleness, docility, and a spaniel-like affection are . . . consistently recommended as the cardinal virtues of the sex; and . . . one writer has declared that it is masculine for a woman to be melancholy. She was created to be the toy of man, his rattle, and it must jingle in his ears whenever, dismissing reason, he chooses to be amused. [*Rights of Woman*, 1792]

Liberty is the mother of virtue, and if women be, by their very constitution, slaves, and not allowed to breathe the sharp invigorating air of freedom, they must ever languish like exotics, and be reckoned beautiful flaws in nature. [*Rights of Woman*, 1792]

Rousseau . . . broaches a doctrine pregnant with mischief and derogatory to the character of supreme wisdom. His ridiculous stories, which tend to prove that girls are *naturally* attentive to their persons, without laying any stress on daily example, are below contempt. . . . I have, probably, had an opportunity of observing more girls in their infancy than J. J. Rousseau—I can recollect my own feelings, and have looked steadily around me; yet, so far from coinciding with him in opinion . . . I will venture to affirm that a girl, whose spirits have not been damped by inactivity, or innocence tainted by false shame, will always be a romp, and the doll will never excite her attention unless confinement allows her no alternative. [*Rights of Woman*, 1792]

Taught . . . that beauty is woman's sceptre, the mind shapes itself to the body, and, roaming round its gilt cage, only seeks to adorn its prison. [*Rights of Woman*, 1792]

Let not men . . . in the pride of power, use the same arguments that tyrannic kings and venal ministers have used, and fallaciously assert that woman ought to be subjected because she always has been so.—But, when man, governed by reasonable laws, enjoys his natural freedom, let him despise woman, if she do not share it with him; and, till that glorious period arrives, in descanting on the folly of the sex, let him not overlook his own. [*Rights of Woman*, 1792]

Inheriting . . . the sovereignty of beauty, [women] have, to maintain their power, resigned the natural rights, which the exercise of reason might have procured them, and chosen rather to be short-lived queens than labour to obtain the sober pleasures that arise from equality. [*Rights of Woman*, 1792]

Novels, music, poetry, and gallantry, all tend to make women the creatures of sensation, and their character is thus formed in the mould of folly during the time they are acquiring accomplishments . . . And will moralists pretend to assert, that this is the condition in which one half the human race should be encouraged to remain, with listless inactivity and stupid acquiescence? Kind instructors! what were we created for? . . . We might as well never have been born, unless it were necessary that we should be created to enable man to acquire the noble privilege of reason, the power of discerning good from evil, whilst we lie down in the dust from whence we were taken, never to rise again. [*Rights of Woman*, 1792]

. . . writers who have most vehemently argued in favour of the superiority of man . . . have laboured to prove, with chivalrous generosity, that the sexes ought not to be compared; man was made to reason, woman to feel: and that together, flesh and spirit, they make the most perfect whole, by blending happily reason and sensibility into one character. [*Rights of Woman*, 1792]

A woman who has lost her honour imagines that she cannot fall lower . . . Losing thus every spur, and having no other means of support, prostitution becomes her only refuge . . . This . . . arises, in a great degree, from the state of idleness in which women are educated, who are always taught to look up to man for a maintenance, and to consider their persons as the proper return for his exertions to support them. [*Rights of Woman*, 1792]

It would almost provoke a smile of contempt, if the vain absurdities of man did not strike us on all sides, to observe how eager men are to degrade the sex from whom they pretend to receive the chief pleasure of life. [*Rights of Woman*, 1792]

. . . it is not against strong, persevering passions, but romantic wavering feelings, that I wish to guard the female heart by exercising the understanding: for these paradisiacal reveries are oftener the effect of idleness than of a lively fancy. [*Rights of Woman*, 1792]

Many poor women maintain their children by the sweat of their brow, and keep together families that the vices of the fathers would have scattered abroad . . . Indeed, the good sense which I have met with, among the poor women who have had few advantages of education, and yet have acted heroically, strongly confirmed me in the opinion that trifling employments have rendered woman a trifler. . . .

who can tell how many generations may be necessary to give vigour to the virtue and talents of the freed posterity of abject slaves? [*Rights of Woman*, 1792]

I shall not lay any great stress on the example of a few women who, from having received a masculine education, have acquired courage and resolution; I only contend that the men who have been placed in similar situations have acquired a similar character—I speak of bodies of men, and that men of genius and talents have started out of a class in which women have never yet been placed. [*Rights of Woman*, 1792]

. . . though the cry of irreligion, or even atheism, be raised against me, I will simply declare that were an angel from heaven to tell me that Moses's beautiful, poetical cosmogony, and the account of the fall of man, were literally true, I could not believe what my reason told me was derogatory to the character of the Supreme Being. [*Rights of Woman*, 1792]

. . . as a sex, men have better tempers than women, because they are occupied by pursuits that interest the head as well as the heart. [*Rights of Woman*, 1792]

Men have superior strength of body; but were it not for mistaken notions of beauty, women would acquire sufficient to enable them to earn their own subsistence, the true definition of independence . . . Let us then, by being allowed to take the same exercise as boys . . . arrive at perfection of body, that we may know how far the natural superiority of man extends. [*Rights of Woman*, 1792]

The pernicious tendency of those books in which the writers insidiously degrade the sex whilst they are prostrate before their personal charms, cannot be too often or too severely exposed. Let us, my dear contemporaries, arise above such narrow prejudices! If wisdom be desirable on its own account, if virtue, to deserve the name, must be founded on knowledge, let us endeavour to strengthen our minds by reflection, till our heads become a balance for our hearts. [*Rights of Woman*, 1792]

A man, or a woman, of any feeling, must always wish to convince a beloved object that it is the caresses of the individual, not the sex, that are received and returned with pleasure; and, that the heart, rather than the senses, is moved. Without this natural delicacy, love becomes a selfish personal gratification that soon degrades the character. [*Rights of Woman*, 1792]

When women are once sufficiently enlightened to discover their real interest, on a grand scale, they will, I am persuaded, be very ready to resign all the prerogatives of love that are not mutual . . . for the calm satisfaction of friendship, and the tender confidence of habitual esteem. [*Rights of Woman*, 1792]

Posterity . . . will remember that Catharine Macaulay was an example of intellectual acquirements supposed to be incompatible with the weakness of her sex. In her style of writing, indeed, no sex appears, for it is, like the sense it conveys, strong and clear. I will not call hers a masculine understanding, because I admit not of such an arrogant assumption of reason; but I contend that . . . the matured fruit of profound thinking was a proof that a woman can acquire judgment, in the full extent of the word. [*Rights of Woman*, 1792]

With ninety-nine men out of a hundred, a very sufficient dash of folly is necessary to render a woman *piquante*, a soft word for desirable . . . One reason, in short, why I wish my whole sex to become wiser is that the foolish ones may not, by their pretty folly, rob those whose sensibility keeps down their vanity of the few roses that afford them some solace in the thorny road of life. [Letter to Imlay: Paris, September 1793]

Considering the care and anxiety a woman must have about a child before it comes into the world, it seems to me, by a *natural right*, to belong to her. . . . Amongst the feathered race, whilst the hen keeps the young warm, her mate stays by to cheer her; but it is sufficient for man to condescend to get a child, in order to claim it.—A man is a tyrant! [Letter to Imlay: Paris, January 1794]

I am particularly attached to [my daughter]—I feel more than a mother's fondness and anxiety, when I reflect on the dependent and oppressed state of her sex. I dread lest she should be forced to sacrifice her heart to her principles, or principles to her heart. . . . I dread to unfold her mind, lest it should render her unfit for the world she is to inhabit—Hapless woman! what a fate is thine! [*Short Residence*, 1795]

Marriage

Wollstonecraft was against marriage on principle, and took every opportunity to denounce it as the institutional enslavement of women. Yet her own life took strange turns.

In France, she took Imlay's name, without benefit of clergy, for political reasons. But after being abandoned by him, the father of her first child, she persuaded Godwin to marry her when she was pregnant with her second—because she was, as Godwin put it, "unwilling, and perhaps with reason, to incur that exclusion from the society of many valuable and excellent individuals, which custom awards in cases of this sort.

"I should have felt an extreme repugnance to the having caused her such an inconvenience. And, after the experiment of seven months . . . there was certainly less hazard to either, in the subjecting ourselves to those consequences which the laws of England annex to the relations of husband and wife."

To their dismay, some shunned them for violating their own principles, while others held Mary's earlier liaison against her.

. . . on many accounts I am averse to any matrimonial tie:—If ever you should venture, may success attend you;—be not too sanguine in your expectations, and you will have less reason to fear a disappointment. [Letter to Jane Arden: Windsor, ca April-June, 1780]

. . . strength of body and mind are sacrificed to libertine notions of beauty, to the desire of establishing themselves—the only way women can rise in the world—by marriage. And . . . when they marry they act as . . . children may be expected to act . . . Surely these weak beings are only fit for a seraglio! Can they be expected to govern a family with judgment, or to take care of the poor babes whom they bring into the world? [*Rights of Woman*, 1792]

. . . alas! husbands, as well as their helpmates, are often only overgrown children; nay, thanks to early debauchery, scarcely men in their outward form—and if the blind lead the blind, one need not come from heaven to tell us the consequence. [*Rights of Woman*, 1792]

The woman who has only been taught to please will soon find that her charms are oblique sunbeams, and that they cannot have much effect on her husband's heart when they are seen every day, when the summer is passed and gone. Will she then have sufficient native energy to look into herself for comfort, and cultivate her dormant faculties? or is it not more rational to expect that she will try to please other men; and, in the emotions raised by the expectation of new conquests, endeavor to forget the mortification her love or pride has received? [*Rights of Woman*, 1792]

. . . the woman who strengthens her body and exercises her mind will, by managing her family and practising various virtues, become the friend, and not the humble dependent, of her husband; and if she, by possessing such substantial qualities, merit his regard, she will not find it necessary to conceal her affection, nor to pretend to an unnatural coldness of constitution to excite her husband's passions. In fact, if we revert to history, we shall find that the women who have distinguished themselves have neither been the most beautiful nor the most gentle of their sex. [*Rights of Woman*, 1792]

If all the faculties of woman's mind are only to be cultivated as they respect her dependence on man; if, when a husband be obtained, she have arrived at her goal, and meanly proud rests satisfied with such a paltry crown, let her grovel contentedly, scarcely raised by her employments above the animal kingdom; but if, struggling for the prize of her high calling, she look beyond the present scene . . . [she] will not model her soul to suit the frailties of her companion, but to bear with them. [*Rights of Woman*, 1792]

I own it frequently happens that women who have fostered a romantic unnatural delicacy of feeling (for example, the herd of Novelists), waste their lives in *imagining* how happy they should have been with a husband who could love them with a fervid increasing affection every day, and all day. But they might as well pine married as single—and would not be a jot more unhappy with a bad husband than longing for a good one. [*Rights of Woman*, 1792]

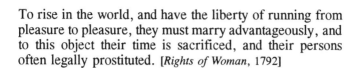

To rise in the world, and have the liberty of running from pleasure to pleasure, they must marry advantageously, and to this object their time is sacrificed, and their persons often legally prostituted. [*Rights of Woman*, 1792]

. . . there are many husbands so devoid of sense and parental affection, that during the first effervescence of voluptuous fondness they refuse to let their wives suckle their children. They are only to dress and live to please them: and love—even innocent love, soon sinks into lasciviousness when the exercise of a duty is sacrificed to its indulgence. [*Rights of Woman*, 1792]

Girls marry merely to *better themselves*, to borrow a significant vulgar phrase, and have such perfect power over their hearts as not to permit themselves to *fall in love* till a man with a superior fortune offers. [*Rights of Woman*, 1792]

Is it unfair to infer that her virtue is built on narrow views and selfishness, who can caress a man, with true feminine softness, the very moment when he treats her tyranically? . . . Let the husband beware of trusting too implicitly to this servile obedience; for if his wife can with winning sweetness caress him when angry . . . she may do the same after parting with a lover. [*Rights of Woman*, 1792]

. . . one grand truth women have yet to learn . . . In the choice of a husband, they should not be led astray by the qualities of a lover—for a lover the husband, even supposing him wise and virtuous, cannot long remain. Were women more rationally educated, could they take a more comprehensive view of things, they would be contented to love but once in their lives; and after marriage calmly let passion subside into friendship—into that tender intimacy which is the best refuge from care. [*Rights of Woman*, 1792]

It is vain to expect virtue from women till they are, in some degree, independent of men; nay, it is vain to expect that strength of natural affection, which would make them good wives and mothers. Whilst they are absolutely dependent on their husbands they will be cunning, mean, and selfish . . . for love is not to be bought . . . its silken wings are instantly shrivelled up when any thing beside a return in kind is sought. [*Rights of Woman*, 1792]

A slavish bondage to parents cramps every faculty of the mind . . . This . . . may in some degree account for the weakness of women; for girls, from various causes, are more kept down by their parents, in every sense of the word, than boys. . . and thus taught slavishly to submit to their parents, they are prepared for the slavery of mar-riage. [*Rights of Woman*, 1792]

. . . marriage will never be held sacred till women, by being brought up with men, are prepared to be their companions rather than their mistresses. [*Rights of Woman*, 1792]

Virtue flies from a house divided against itself—and a whole legion of devils take up their residence there. The affection of husbands and wives cannot be pure when they have so few sentiments in common, and when so little confidence is established at home, as must be the case

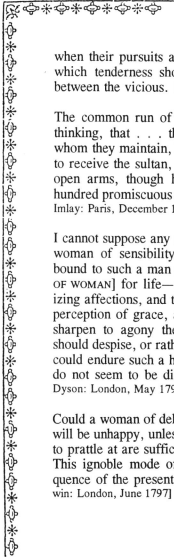

when their pursuits are so different. That intimacy from which tenderness should flow, will not, cannot subsist between the vicious. [*Rights of Woman*, 1792]

The common run of men have such an ignoble way of thinking, that . . . they suppose the wife, slave rather, whom they maintain, has no right to complain, and ought to receive the sultan, whenever he deigns to return, with open arms, though his have been polluted by half an hundred promiscuous amours during his absence. [Letter to Imlay: Paris, December 1794]

I cannot suppose any situation more distressing than for a woman of sensibility, with an improving mind, to be bound to such a man as I have described [in THE WRONGS OF WOMAN] for life—obliged to renounce all the humanizing affections, and to avoid cultivating her taste lest her perception of grace, and refinement of sentiment should sharpen to agony the pangs of disappointment . . . I should despise, or rather call her an ordinary woman, who could endure such a husband as I have sketched—yet you do not seem to be disgusted with him!!! [Letter to George Dyson: London, May 1797]

Could a woman of delicacy seduce and marry a fool? She will be unhappy, unless a situation in life and a good table to prattle at are sufficient to fill up the void of affection. This ignoble mode of rising in the world is the consequence of the present system of education. [Letter to Godwin: London, June 1797]

Child Care and Education

Wollstonecraft hammered away at the importance of educating girls to be not just wives, but rounded, self-respecting citizens. Refuting much of the theoretical literature of Rousseau and other experts, she drew on her experience as a teacher and governess, as well as on her own childhood, to bolster her arguments. And she advocated pedagogical methods so in advance of her own time that many are still being argued today.

The suckling of a child . . . excites the warmest glow of tenderness—Its dependant, helpless state produces an affection which may properly be termed maternal. I have even felt it, when I have seen a mother perform that office; and am of the opinion, that maternal tenderness arises quite as much from habit as instinct. [*Education of Daughters*, The Nursery, 1787]

The usual mode of acting is complying with the humours sometimes, and contradicting them at others . . . This the infant finds out earlier than can be imagined, and it gives rise to an affection devoid of respect. Uniformity of conduct is the only feasible method of creating both. . . . yet a rigid style of behaviour is by no means to be adopted; on the contrary . . . it is only in the years of childhood that the happiness of a human being depends entirely on others—and to embitter those years by needless restraint is cruel. To conciliate affection, affection must be shown, and little proofs of it ought always to be given—let them not appear weaknesses, and they will sink deep into the young mind and call forth its most amiable propensities. [*Education of Daughters*, The Nursery, 1787]

In the nursery . . . they are taught to speak; and there they not only hear nonsense, but that nonsense retailed in such silly, affected tones as must disgust;—yet these are the tones which the child first imitates . . . but afterwards they are not easily got the better of—nay, many women always retain the pretty prattle of the nursery, and do not forget to lisp, when they have learnt to languish. [*Education of Daughters*, The Nursery, 1787]

It is, in my opinion, a well-proved fact, that principles of truth are innate. . . . and artful sophistry can only blunt those feelings which nature has implanted in us as instinctive guards to virtue. Dissimulation and cunning will soon drive all other good qualities before them, and deprive the mind of that beautiful simplicity which can never be too much cherished. [*Education of Daughters*, Moral Discipline, 1787]

Children should be permitted to enter into conversation; but it requires great discernment to find out such subjects as will gradually improve them. [*Education of Daughters*, Moral Discipline, 1787]

Intellectual improvements, like the growth and formation of the body, must be gradual—yet there is no reason why the mind should lie fallow, while its "frail tenement" is imperceptibly fitting itself for a more reasonable inhabitant. . . . Whenever a child asks a question, it should always have a reasonable answer given it. [*Education of Daughters*, Moral Discipline, 1787]

As to prejudices, the first notions we have deserve that name; for it is not till we begin to waver in our opinions that we exert our reason to examine them—and then, if they are received, they may be called our own. [*Education of Daughters*, Moral Discipline, 1787]

It is of more use than can be conceived, for a child to learn to compare things that are similar in some respects, and different in others. I wish them to be taught to think—thinking, indeed, is a severe exercise . . . Not that I would have them make long reflections; for when they do not arise from experience, they are mostly absurd. [*Education of Daughters*, Moral Discipline, 1787]

I have known children who could repeat things in the order they learnt them, that were quite at a loss when put out of the beaten track. If the understanding is not exercised, the memory will be employed to little purpose. [*Education of Daughters*, Exterior Accomplishments, 1787]

Young people are very apt to substitute words for sentiments, and clothe mean thoughts in pompous diction. Industry and time are necessary to cure this, and will often do it. Children should be led into correspondences, and

methods adopted to make them write down their sentiments, and they should be prevailed on to relate the stories
they have read in their own words. Writing well is of
great consequence in life . . . as it teaches a person to
arrange their thoughts, and digest them. [*Education of
Daughters*, The Fine Arts, 1787]

A relish for reading . . . should be cultivated very early
in life. . . . Reading is the most rational employment, if
people seek food for the understanding, and do not read
merely to remember words or with a view to quote
celebrated authors . . . . Judicious books enlarge the mind
and improve the heart. . . . I do not mean to recommend
books of an abstracted or grave cast. . . . Reason strikes
most forcibly when illustrated by the brilliancy of fancy.
[*Education of Daughters*, Reading, 1787]

I recommend the mind's being put into a proper train, and
then left to itself. Fixed rules cannot be given. . . . The
mind is not, cannot be created by the teacher, though it
may be cultivated, and its real powers found out. [*Education
of Daughters*, Reading, 1787]

. . . knowledge should be gradually imparted, and flow
more from example than teaching; example directly ad-
dresses the senses . . . the object [which] education should
have constantly in view, and over which we have most
power. [*Original Stories*, Preface, 1788]

Contending for the rights of woman, my main argument
is built on this simple principle, that if she be not prepared
by education to become the companion of man, she will

stop the progress of knowledge and virtue; for truth must be common to all, or it will be inefficacious with respect to its influence on general practice. [*Rights of Woman* 1792]

By individual education, I mean . . . such an attention to a child as will slowly sharpen the senses, form the temper, regulate the passions as they begin to ferment, and set the understanding to work before the body arrives at maturity. [*Rights of Woman*, 1792]

Men and women must be educated, in a great degree, by the opinions and manners of the society they live in. In every age there has been a stream of popular opinion that has carried all before it, and given a family character, as it were, to the century. It may then fairly be inferred, that, till society be differently constituted, much cannot be expected from education. [*Rights of Woman*, 1792]

. . . a proper education, or, to speak with more precision, a well stored mind, would enable a woman to support a single life with dignity. [*Rights of Woman*, 1792]

I will allow that bodily strength seems to give man a natural superiority over woman; and this is the only solid basis on which the superiority of the sex can be built. But I still insist that not only the virtue but the *knowledge* of the two sexes should be the same in nature, if not in degree, and that women, considered not only as moral, but rational creatures, ought to endeavour to acquire human virtues (or perfections) by the *same* means as men, instead of being educated like a fanciful kind of *half* being. [*Rights of Woman*, 1792]

. . . the first care of those mothers or fathers, who really attend to the education of females, should be, if not to strengthen the body, at least, not to destroy the constitution by mistaken notions of beauty and female excellence; nor should girls ever be allowed to imbibe the pernicious notion that a defect can, by any chemical process of reasoning, become an excellence. [*Rights of Woman*, 1792]

Throughout the whole animal kingdom every young creature requires almost continual exercise, and the infancy of children . . . should be passed in harmless gambols . . . But . . . to preserve personal beauty, woman's glory! the limbs and faculties are cramped with worse than Chinese bands, and the sedentary life which they are condemned to live, whilst boys frolic in the open air, weakens the muscles and relaxes the nerves.—As for Rousseau's remarks . . . that they have naturally, that is from their birth, independent of education, a fondness for dolls, dressing, and talking—they are so puerile as not to merit a serious refutation. [*Rights of Woman*, 1792]

. . . from their infancy women should either be shut up like eastern princes, or educated in such a manner as to be able to think and act for themselves. . . . for how can a rational being be ennobled by any thing that is not obtained by its

The power (
sive conclus
acquirement
edge. . . . 1
en; but . . .

tion of the understanding more difficult in the female than the male world. [*Rights of Woman*, 1792]

"Educate women like men," says Rousseau, "and the more they resemble our sex the less power will they have over us." This is the very point I aim at. I do not wish them to have power over men; but over themselves. [*Rights of Woman*, 1792]

. . . perhaps, in the education of both sexes, the most difficult task is so to adjust instruction as not to narrow the understanding . . . nor to dry up the feelings by employing the mind in investigations remote from life. [*Rights of Woman*, 1792]

Severity is frequently the most certain as well as the most sublime proof of affection; and the want of this power over the feelings . . . is the reason why so many fond mothers spoil their children, and has made it questionable whether negligence or indulgence be most hurtful; but I am inclined to think that the latter has done most harm. [*Rights of Woman*, 1792]

. . . a person of genius is the most improper person to be employed in education, public or private. Minds of this rare species see things too much in masses, and seldom, if ever, have a good temper. [*Rights of Woman*, 1792]

. . . we expect more from instruction, than mere instruction can produce: for, instead of preparing young people to encounter the evils of life with dignity, and to acquire wisdom and virtue by the exercise of their own faculties, precepts are heaped upon precepts, and blind obedience required, when conviction should be brought home to reason. [*Rights of Woman*, 1792]

. . . men expect from education, what education cannot give. A sagacious parent or tutor may strengthen the body and sharpen the instruments by which the child is to gather knowledge; but the honey must be the reward of the individual's own industry. It is almost as absurd to attempt to make a youth wise by the experience of another, as to expect the body to grow strong by the exercise which is only talked of, or seen. [*Rights of Woman*, 1792]

In order to open their faculties, they should be excited to think for themselves; and this can only be done by mixing a number of children together, and making them jointly pursue the same objects. A child very soon contracts a benumbing indolence of mind, which he has seldom sufficient vigour afterwards to shake off, when he only asks a question instead of seeking for information, and then relies implicitly on the answer he receives. With his equals in age this could never be the case, and the subjects of inquiry, though they might be influenced, would not be entirely under the direction of men, who frequently damp, if not destroy abilities, by bringing them forward too hastily. [*Rights of Woman*, 1792]

The only way to avoid two extremes equally injurious to morality, would be to contrive some way of combining a public and private education. Thus, to make men citizens, two natural steps might be taken which seem directly to lead to the desired point; for the domestic affections, that first open the heart to the various modifications of humanity, would be cultivated, whilst the children were nevertheless allowed to spend a great part of their time, on terms of equality, with other children. [*Rights of Woman*, 1792]

. . . to improve both sexes they ought, not only in private families, but in public schools, to be educated together. If marriage be the cement of society, mankind should all be educated after the same model. . . . The school for the younger children . . . ought to be absolutely free and open to all classes. . . . And to prevent any of the distinctions of vanity, they should be dressed alike, and all obliged to submit to the same discipline. [*Rights of Woman*, 1792]

In public schools, women, to guard against the errors of ignorance, should be taught the elements of anatomy and medicine . . . It is likewise proper . . . to make women acquainted with the anatomy of the mind, by allowing the sexes to associate together in every pursuit; and by leading them to observe the progress of the human understanding in the improvement of the sciences and arts; never forgetting the science of morality, or the study of the political history of mankind. [*Rights of Woman*, 1792]

National Character

Wollstonecraft's aim in observing and analyzing the cultural differences in the countries she visited was "to take such a dispassionate view of men as will lead me to form a just idea of the nature of man."

For a young woman of limited means, she spent what must have been an unusual amount of time abroad. She went to Portugal to care for her dearest friend, Fanny Blood, lived and traveled in Ireland as a governess, made her home in France before and during her affair with Imlay, and toured the Scandinavian countries as his representative.

The French, who admit more of mind into their notions of beauty, give the preference to women of thirty. . . they allow women to be in their most perfect state when vivacity gives place to reason and to that majestic seriousness of character which marks maturity. [*Rights of Woman,* 1792]

I have not had any reason to alter the opinion which I formed of the French from reading their history & memoirs, yet I must make one observation to you, for it has forcibly struck me—those who wish to live for themselves without close friendship or affection ought to live in Paris, for they have the pleasantest way of whiling away time— and their urbanity, like their furniture, is *très commode*. [Letter to Eliza: Paris, January 1793]

All the affection I have for the French is for the whole nation, and it seems to be a little honey spread over all the bread I eat in their land. [Letter to Ruth Barlow: Paris, February 1793]

It is necessary, perhaps, for an observer of mankind to guard as carefully the remembrance of the first impression made by a nation, as by a countenance; because we imperceptibly lose sight of the national character, when we become more intimate with individuals. [Letter to Joseph Johnson: Paris, February 1793 (published posthumously)]

The Swedes pique themselves on their politeness; but far from being the polish of a cultivated mind, it consists merely of tiresome forms and ceremonies . . . their overacted civility . . . has a contrary effect than what is intended; so that I could not help reckoning the peasantry the politest people of Sweden, who, only aiming at pleasing you, never think of being admired for their behaviour. [*Short Residence*, 1795]

. . . the manners of a people are best discriminated in the country. The inhabitants of the capital are all of the same genus; for the varieties in the species we must, therefore, search where the habitations of men are so separated as to allow the difference of climate to have its natural effect. [*Short Residence*, 1795]

. . . most writers of travels . . . are eager to give a national character; which is rarely just, because they do not discriminate the natural from the acquired difference. The natural . . . will be found to consist merely in the degree of vivacity or thoughtfulness, pleasure, or pain, inspired by the climate; whilst the varieties which the forms of government, including religion, produce, are much more numerous and unstable. . . . The most essential service . . . that authors could render to society would be to promote inquiry and discussion, instead of making those dogmatical assertions which only appear calculated to gird the human mind round with imaginary circles, like the paper globe which represents the one he inhabits. This spirit of inquiry is the characteristic of the present century, from which the succeeding will . . . receive a great accumulation of knowledge; and doubtless its diffusion will in a great measure destroy the factitious national characters which have been supposed permanent, though only rendered so by the permanency of ignorance. [*Short Residence*, 1795]

. . . in my general observations, I do not pretend to sketch a national character; but merely to note the present state of morals and manners, as I trace the progress of the world's improvement. Because, during my residence in different countries, my principal object has been to take such a dispassionate view of men as will lead me to form a just idea of the nature of man. [*Short Residence*, 1795]

The French Revolution

"The French revolution," Godwin wrote in his *Memoirs* of the author, produced "a conspicuous effect in the progress of Mary's reflections. The prejudices of her early years suffered a vehement concussion. Her respect for establishments was undermined."

She already had a modest reputation as a writer when she exploded in 1790 with A VINDICATION OF THE RIGHTS OF MEN, her vitriolic reply to Edmund Burke's *Reflections on the Revolution in France.* That this 31-year-old *woman* chose to refute, on a very personal level, the arguments of a respected statesman twice her age, was surely the height of chutzpah.

The publication of this book propelled her, according to Godwin, into the "rank which from this time she held in the lists of literature. . . . Mary, full of sentiments of liberty, and impressed with a warm interest in the struggle that was now going on, seized her pen in the first burst of indignation, an emotion of which she was strongly susceptible. . . . Marked as it is with the vehemence and impetuousness of its eloquence, it is certainly chargeable with a too contemptuous and intemperate treatment of the great man against whom its attack is directed. But this circumstance was not injurious to the success of the publication."

It wasn't until late 1792 that Wollstonecraft herself went to France to witness the upheaval at first hand. Though by 1794 the "calamitous horrours produced by desperate and enraged factions" shocked and saddened her, she wrote her HISTORICAL AND MORAL VIEW . . . OF THE FRENCH REVOLUTION from the long-range perspective of "the uncontaminated mass of the French nation, whose minds begin to grasp the sentiments of freedom."

Time only will shew whether the general censure . . . and the unmerited contempt that you have ostentatiously displayed of the National Assembly, is founded on reason . . . or the spawn of envy. Time may shew that this obscure throng knew more of the human heart and of legislation than the profligates of rank, emasculated by hereditary effeminacy. [*Rights of Men*, 1790]

. . . in setting a constitution that involved the happiness of millions . . . it was, perhaps, necessary to have a higher model in view than the *imagined* virtues of their forefathers . . . Why was it a duty to repair an ancient castle, built in barbarous ages . . . when a simple structure might be raised on the foundation of experience? [*Rights of Men*, 1790]

. . . if this grand example is set by an assembly of unlettered clowns, if they can produce a crisis that may involve the fate of Europe, and more than Europe, you must allow us to respect unsophisticated common sense. . . . In order that liberty should have a firm foundation, an acquaintance with the world would naturally lead cool men to conclude that it must be laid . . . either by *poor* men or philosophers . . . I am afraid that human nature is still in such a weak state, that the abolition of titles, the corner-stone of despotism, could only have been the work of men who had no titles to sacrifice. [*Rights of Men*, 1790]

. . . let me beg you not to mix with the shallow herd who throw an odium on immutable principles, because some of the mere instrument of the revolution were too sharp.— Children of any growth will do mischief when they meddle with edged tools. It is to be lamented that *as yet* the billows of public opinion are only to be moved forward by the strong wind, the squally gusts of passion; but if nations be educated by their governments, it is vain to expect much reason till the system of education becomes more reasonable. [Letter to William Roscoe: London, November 1792]

. . . my spirits are fatigued with endeavouring to form a just opinion of public affairs— The day after to morrow I expect to see the king at the bar—and the consequences that will follow I am almost afraid to anticipate. [Letter to Everina: Paris, December 1792]

. . . the prudent precautions taken by the National Convention to prevent a tumult made me suppose that the dogs of faction would not dare to bark, much less to bite, however true to their scent; and I was not mistaken; for the

citizens . . . are returning home with composed counte-
nances, shouldering their arms. . . . For the first time
since I entered France, I bowed to the majesty of the people, and respected the propriety of behaviour so perfectly
in unison with my own feelings. [Letter to Joseph Johnson:
Paris, December 1792]

You may think it too soon to form an opinion of the future
government, yet it is impossible to avoid hazarding some
conjectures, when every thing whispers me, that names,
not principles, are changed, and when I see that the turn
of the tide has left the dregs of the old system to corrupt
the new. For the same pride of office, the same desire of
power are still visible; with this aggravation, that, fearing
to return to obscurity after having but just acquired a
relish for distinction, each hero, or philosopher, for all are
dubbed with these new titles, endeavours to make hay
while the sun shines; and every petty municipal officer,
become the idol, or rather the tyrant of the day, stalks like
a cock on a dunghil. [Letter to Joseph Johnson: Paris, 1793]

I really believe that Europe will be in a state of convulsion
during half a century at least. [Letter to Imlay: Paris, January
1794]

It is impossible for you to have any idea of the impression
the sad scenes I have been a witness to have left on my
mind. The climate of France is uncommonly fine, the
country pleasant, and there is a degree of ease, and even
simplicity, in the manners of the common people, which
attaches me to them— Still, death and misery, in every
shape of terrour, haunts this devoted country— I certainly

am glad that I came to France, because I never could have had else a just opinion of the most extraordinary event that has ever been recorded. [Letter to Everina: Havre, March 1794]

The French will carry all before them—but, my God, how many victims fall beneath the sword and the Guillotine! My blood runs cold, and I sicken at thoughts of a Revolution which costs so much blood and bitter tears. [Letter to Ruth Barlow: Havre, July 1794]

The rapid changes, the violent, the base, and nefarious assassinations, which have clouded the vivid prospect that began to spread a ray of joy and gladness over the gloomy horizon of oppression, cannot fail to chill the sympathizing bosom, and palsy intellectual vigour. . . . Contemplating then these stupendous events with the cool eye of observation, the judgement, difficult to be preserved unwarped under the pressure of the calamitous horrours produced by desperate and enraged factions, will continually perceive that it is the uncontaminated mass of the French nation, whose minds begin to grasp the sentiments of freedom, that has secured the equilibrium of the state. [*Revolution*, 1794]

Reason has, at last, shown her captivating face, beaming with benevolence; and it will be impossible for the dark hand of despotism again to obscure its radiance, or the lurking dagger of subordinate tyrants to reach her bosom. [*Revolution*, 1794]

. . . [the queen] seldom failed to carry her point when she endeavoured to gain an ascendancy over the mind of an individual. Over the king she acquired unbounded sway, when, managing the disgust she had for his person, she made him pay a kingly price for her favours. A court is the best school in the world for actors; it was very natural then for her to become a complete actress, and an adept in all the arts of coquetry that debauch the mind, whilst they render the person alluring. [*Revolution*, 1794]

Down fell the temple of despotism; but—despotism has not been buried in its ruins!—Unhappy country!—when will thy children cease to tear thy bosom?—When will a change of opinion, producing a change of morals, render thee truly free?—When will truth give life to real magnanimity, and justice place equality on a stable seat?—When will thy sons trust, because they deserve to be trusted; and private virtue become the guarantee of patriotism? Ah!—when will thy government become the most perfect, because thy citizens are the most virtuous! [*Revolution*, 1794]

The Parisians were now [October 1789] brooding over the wrongs they had heretofore only enumerated in a song; and changing ridicule into invective, all called for redress, looking for a degree of public happiness immediately, which could not be attained, and ought not to have been expected, before an alteration in the national character seconded the new system of government. [*Revolution*, 1794]

The deprivation of natural, equal, civil and political rights, reduced the most cunning of the lower orders to practise fraud, and the rest to habits of stealing, audacious robberies and murders. And why? because the rich and poor were separated into bands of tyrants and slaves, and the retaliation of slaves is always terrible. In short, every sacred feeling, moral and divine, has been obliterated, and the dignity of man sullied, by a system of policy and jurisprudence as repugnant to reason, as at variance with humanity. . . . When justice, or the law, is so partial, the day of retribution will come with the red sky of vengeance, to confound the innocent with the guilty. [*Revolution*, 1794]

The liberty of the press will produce a great effect here—the *cry of blood will not be vain!* Some more monsters will perish—and the Jacobins are conquered. Yet I almost fear the last flap of the tail of the beast. [Letter to Imlay: Paris, October 1794]

. . . the Norwegians . . . wish well to the republican cause; and follow, with the most lively interest, the successes of the French arms. So determined were they, in fact, to excuse every thing disgracing the struggle of freedom by admitting the tyrant's plea, necessity, that I could hardly persuade them that Robespierre was a monster. [*Short Residence*, 1795]

Social/Economic/Political Justice

In both of her VINDICATIONS, as well as in her later writings, Wollstonecraft consistently stressed the interrelationship of human rights, economic conditions, and political corruption in perpetuating the oppression of humankind in general and womankind in particular.

Sensibility is the *manie* of the day, and compassion the virtue which is to cover a multitude of vices, whilst justice is left to mourn in sullen silence, and balance truth in vain. [*Rights of Men*, 1790]

The birthright of man . . . is such a degree of liberty, civil and religious, as is compatible with the liberty of the other individuals whom he is united with in a social compact. Liberty, in this simple . . . sense . . . is a fair idea that has never yet received a form in the various governments that have been established on our beauteous globe; the demon of property has ever been at hand to encroach on the sacred rights of men. [*Rights of Men*, 1790]

Is it necessary to repeat, that there are rights which we received, at our birth, as men, when we were raised above

the brute creation by the power of improving ourselves—and that we receive these not from our forefathers,
but from God? [*Rights of Men*, 1790]

. . . it is only the property of the rich that is secure; the
man who lives by the sweat of his brow has no asylum
from oppression. . . . it is a farce to pretend that a man
fights *for his country, his hearth, or his altars,* when he
has neither liberty nor property. [*Rights of Men*, 1790]

. . . your tears are reserved . . . for the downfall of
queens, whose rank throws a graceful veil over vices that
degrade humanity; but the distress of many industrious
mothers, whose *helpmates* have been torn from them, and
the hungry cry of helpless babes, were vulgar sorrows that
could not move your commiseration though they might
extort alms. [*Rights of Men*, 1790]

. . . we should not forget how much we owe to chance
that our inheritance was not Mahometism; and that the
iron hand of destiny, in the shape of deeply-rooted authority, has not suspended the sword of destruction over our
heads. [*Rights of Men*, 1790]

. . . you must have seen the clogged wheels of corruption
continually oiled by the sweat of the laborious poor,
squeezed out of them by unceasing taxation. You must
have discovered that the majority in the House of Commons was often purchased by the crown, and that the
people were oppressed by the influence of their own
money, extorted by the venial voice of a packed representation. [*Rights of Men*, 1790]

A brutal attachment to children has appeared most conspicuous in parents who have treated them like slaves, and
demanded due homage for all the property they transferred
to them, during their lives. It has led them to force their
children to break the most sacred ties; to do violence to a
natural impulse, and run into legal prostitution to increase
wealth or shun poverty. [*Rights of Men*, 1790]

Property . . . should be fluctuating, or it is an everlasting
rampart, a barbarous feudal institution, that enables the
rich to overpower talents and depress virtue. . . . The
only security of property that nature authorises and reason
sanctions is the right a man has to enjoy the acquisitions
which his talents or industry have acquired; and happy
would it be for the world if there was no other road to
wealth or honour. [*Rights of Men*, 1790]

I reverence the rights of men.—Sacred rights! for which
I acquire a more profound respect, the more I look into
my own mind. [*Rights of Men*, 1790]

Experience, I believe, will show that sordid interest, or li-
centious thoughtlessness, is the spring of action at most
elections. . . . So far from the people being habitually
convinced of the sanctity of the charge they are confer-
ring, the venality of their votes must admonish them that
they have no right to expect disinterested conduct. [*Rights
of Men*, 1790]

That the British House of Commons is filled with every
thing illustrious in rank, in descent, in hereditary and
acquired opulence, may be true,—but that it contains every

thing respectable in talents, in military, civil, naval, and political distinction, is very problematical. [*Rights of Men*, 1790]

The liberty of the rich has its ensigns armorial to puff the individual out with unsubstantial honours; but where are blazoned the struggles of virtuous poverty? [*Rights of Men*, 1790]

On the natural principles of justice I build my plea for disseminating the property artfully said to be appropriated to religious purposes, but, in reality, to support idle tyrants . . . the clergy would be rendered both more virtuous and useful by being put more on a par with each other, and the mass of the people it was their duty to instruct. [*Rights of Men*, 1790]

According to the limited view of timid, or interested politicians, an abolition of the infernal slave trade would not only be unsound policy, but a flagrant infringement of the laws (though they have been allowed to become infamous) that authorise the planters to purchase their estates. But is it not consonant with justice, with the common principles of humanity, not to mention Christianity, to abolish this abominable inveterate mischief? [*Rights of Men*, 1790]

Benevolence is a very amiable specious quality; yet the aversion which men feel to accept a right as a favour should rather be extolled as a vestige of native dignity, than stigmatized as the odious offspring of ingratitude. [*Rights of Men*, 1790]

It may be confidently asserted that no man chooses evil, because it is evil; he only mistakes it for happiness, the good he seeks. [*Rights of Men*, 1790]

It is, Sir, *possible* to render the poor happier in this world, without depriving them of the consolation which you gratuitously grant them in the next. They have a right to more comfort than they at present enjoy; and more comfort might be afforded them, without encroaching on the pleasure of the rich. [*Rights of Men*, 1790]

Why cannot large estates be divided into small farms? these dwellings would indeed grace our land. Why are huge forests still allowed to stretch out with idle pomp and all the indolence of Eastern grandeur? Why do the brown wastes meet the traveller's view, when men want work? . . . Why might not the industrious peasant be allowed to steal a farm from the heath? . . . In this great city, that proudly rears its head, and boasts of its population and commerce, how much misery lurks in pestilential corners . . . ! Where is the eye that marks these evils, more gigantic than any of the infringements of property which you piously deprecate? [*Rights of Men*, 1790]

Man preys on man; and you mourn for the idle tapestry that decorated a gothic pile, and the dronish bell that summoned the fat priest to prayer. . . . Hell stalks abroad;—the lash resounds on the slave's naked sides; and the sick wretch, who can no longer earn the sour bread of unremitting labour, steals to a ditch to bid the world a long good night . . . Such misery demands more than tears. [*Rights of Men*, 1790]

The desire of dazzling by riches, the most certain pre-eminence that man can obtain, the pleasure of commanding flattering sycophants, and many other . . . calculations of doting self-love, have all contributed to overwhelm the mass of mankind, and make liberty a convenient handle for mock patriotism. [*Rights of Woman*, 1792]

. . . one power should not be thrown down to exalt another—for all power inebriates weak man. [*Rights of Woman*, 1792]

. . . every profession in which great subordination of rank constitutes its power is highly injurious to morality. . . . Society, therefore, as it becomes more enlightened, should be very careful not to establish bodies of men who must necessarily be made foolish or vicious by the very constitution of their profession. [*Rights of Woman*, 1792]

. . . the very constitution of civil governments has put almost insuperable obstacles in the way to prevent the cultivation of the female understanding. [*Rights of Woman*, 1792]

"He that hath wife and children," says Lord Bacon, "hath given hostages to fortune; for they are impediments to great enterprises, either of virtue or mischief. Certainly the best works, and of greatest merit for the public, have proceeded from the unmarried or childless men." I say the same of women. But the welfare of society is not built on extraordinary exertions; and were it more reasonably organized, there would be still less need of great abilities, or heroic virtues. [*Rights of Woman*, 1792]

Riches and honours prevent a man from enlarging his understanding, and enervate all his powers by reversing the order of nature, which has ever made true pleasure the reward of labour. [*Rights of Woman*, 1792]

From the respect paid to property, flow, as from a poisoned fountain, most of the evils and vices which render this world such a dreary scene to the contemplative mind. . . . One class presses on another; for all are aiming to procure respect on account of their property . . . Men neglect the duties incumbent on man, yet are treated like demi-gods; religion is also separated from morality by a ceremonial veil, yet men wonder that the world is almost, literally speaking, a den of sharpers or oppressors. [*Rights of Woman*, 1792]

There must be more equality established in society . . . and this virtuous equality will not rest firmly even when founded on a rock, if one half of mankind be chained to its bottom by fate, for they will be continually undermining it through ignorance or pride. [*Rights of Woman*, 1792]

The laws respecting woman . . . make an absurd unit of a man and his wife; and then, by the easy transition of only considering him as responsible, she is reduced to a mere cypher. [*Rights of Woman*, 1792]

. . . surely the present system of war has little connection with virtue of any denomination, being rather the school of *finesse* and effeminacy, than of fortitude. Yet, if defensive war, the only justifiable war . . . were alone to be adopted as just and glorious, the true heroism of antiquity might again animate female bosoms.—But fair and softly, gentle reader, male or female, do not alarm thyself . . . I am not going to advise them to turn their distaff into a musket, though I sincerely wish to see the bayonet converted into a pruning-hook. [*Rights of Woman*, 1792]

. . . though . . . women in the common walks of life are called to fulfil the duties of wives and mothers . . . women of a superiour cast have not a road open by which they can pursue more extensive plans of usefulness and independence. I may excite laughter, by dropping an hint . . . that women ought to have representatives, instead of being arbitrarily governed without having any direct share allowed them in the deliberations of government. But, as the whole system of representation is now, in this country, only a convenient handle for despotism, they need not complain, for they are as well represented as a numerous class of hard working mechanics, who pay for the support of royalty when they can scarcely stop their children's mouths with bread. [*Rights of Woman*, 1792]

But what have women to do in society? . . . Women might certainly study the art of healing, and be physicians as well as nurses. . . They might, also, study politics, and settle their benevolence on the broadest basis . . . Business of various kinds, they might likewise pursue, if they were educated in a more orderly manner, which might save many from common and legal prostitution. . . . is not that government then very defective, and very unmindful of the happiness of one half of its members, that does not provide for honest, independent women, by encouraging them to fill respectable stations? . . . How many women thus waste life away the prey of discontent, who might have practised as physicians, regulated a farm, managed a shop, and stood erect, supported by their own industry. [*Rights of Woman*, 1792]

Those writers are particularly useful . . . who make man feel for man . . . I appeal to their understandings; and, as a fellow-creature, claim, in the name of my sex, some interest in their hearts. I entreat them to assist to emancipate their companion, to make her a *help meet* for them! Would men but generously snap our chains . . . they would find us more observant daughters, more affectionate sisters, more faithful wives, more reasonable mothers—in a word, better citizens. [*Rights of Woman*, 1792]

. . . a right always includes a duty, and I think it may, likewise, fairly be inferred, that they forfeit the right, who do not fulfil the duty. [*Rights of Woman*, 1792]

. . . great men seem to start up, as great revolutions occur, at proper intervals, to restore order, and to blow aside the clouds that thicken over the face of truth; but let more reason and virtue prevail in society, and these strong winds would not be necessary. [*Rights of Woman*, 1792]

Let women share the rights and she will emulate the virtues of man; for she must grow more perfect when emancipated, or justify the authority that chains such a weak being to her duty.—If the latter, it will be expedient to open a fresh trade with Russia for whips; a present, which a father should always make to his son-in-law on his wedding day. [*Rights of Woman*, 1792]

. . . if really equality should ever take place in society, the man who is employed and gives a just equivalent for the money he receives will not behave with the obsequiousness of a servant. [Letter to Mary Hays: London, November 1792]

That there is a superiority of natural genius among men does not admit of dispute; and that in countries the most free there will always be distinctions proceeding from superiority of judgment . . . But it is a palpable errour to suppose that men of every class are not equally susceptible of common improvement; if therefore it be the contrivance of any government, to preclude from a chance of improvement the greater part of the citizens of the state, it can be considered in no other light than as a monstrous tyranny, a barbarous oppression, equally injurious to the two parties, though in different ways. For all the advantages of civilization cannot be felt, unless it pervades the whole mass, humanizing every description of men—and then it is the first of blessings, the true perfection of man. [*Revolution*, 1794]

The ferocity of the savage is of a distinct nature from that of the degenerate slaves of tyrants. One murders from mistaken notions of courage; yet he respects his enemy in proportion to his fortitude, and contempt of death: the other assassinates without remorse, whilst his trembling nerves betray the weakness of his affrighted soul at every appearance of danger. Among the former, men are respected according to their abilities; consequently idle drones are driven out of this society; but among the latter, men are raised to honours and employments in proportion as a talent for intrigue, the sure proof of littleness of mind, has rendered them servile. [*Revolution*, 1794]

Much public virtue cannot be expected till every employment, putting perquisites out of the question, has a salary sufficient to reward industry, whilst none are so great as to permit the possessor to remain idle. It is this want of proportion between profit and labour which debases men. [*Short Residence*, 1795]

I . . . found myself in the midst of a group of lawyers, of different descriptions. My head turned round, my heart grew sick, as I regarded visages deformed by vice; and listened to accounts of chicanery that were continually embroiling the ignorant. . . it is these men, whose wits have been sharpened by knavery, who here undermine morality, confounding right and wrong. [*Short Residence*, 1795]

You may think me too severe on commerce; but from the manner it is at present carried on, little can be advanced in favour of a pursuit that wears out the most sacred principles of humanity and rectitude. [*Short Residence*, 1795]

England and America owe their liberty to commerce, which created a new species of power to undermine the feudal system. But let them beware of the consequence; the tyranny of wealth is still more galling and debasing than that of rank. [*Short Residence*, 1795]

I am persuaded that till capital punishments be entirely abolished, executions ought to have every appearance of horrour given to them; instead of being, as they are now, a scene of amusement for the gaping crowd, where sympathy is quickly effaced by curiosity. I have always been of the opinion that the allowing actors to die, in the presence of the audience, has an immoral tendency; but trifling when compared with the ferocity acquired by viewing the reality as a show . . . Consequently executions, far from being useful examples to the survivors, have . . . a quite contrary effect, by hardening the heart they ought to terrify. Besides, the fear of an ignominious death, I believe, never deterred any one from the commission of a crime; because, in committing it, the mind is roused to activity about present circumstances. It is a game at hazard, at which all expect the turn of the die in their own favour, never reflecting on the chance of ruin, till it comes. [*Short Residence*, 1795]

. . . the same energy of character, which renders a man a daring villain, would have rendered him useful to society, had that society been well organized. When a strong mind is not disciplined by cultivation, it is a sense of injustice that renders it unjust. [*Short Residence*, 1795]

. . . I do not think the situation of the poor in England is much, if at all, superiour to that of the same class in different parts of the world . . . for at present the accumulation of national wealth only increases the cares of the poor, and hardens the hearts of the rich, in spite of the highly extolled rage for alms-giving. . . . I have always been an enemy to what is termed charity, because timid bigots, endeavouring thus to cover their *sins*, do violence to justice, till, acting the demi-god, they forget that they are men. And there are others . . . whose benevolence is merely tyranny in disguise. [*Short Residence*, 1795]

. . . I have had an opportunity of peeping behind the scenes of what are vulgarly termed great affairs, only to discover the mean machinery which has directed many transactions of moment. The sword has been merciful, compared with the depredations made on human life by contractors, and by the swarm of locusts who have battened on the pestilence they spread abroad. These men, like the owners of negro ships, never smell on their money the blood by which it has been gained, but sleep quietly in their beds, terming such occupations *lawful callings*. [*Short Residence*, 1795]

. . . the gigantic evils of despotism and anarchy have in a great measure vanished before the meliorating manners of Europe. Innumerable evils still remain, it is true, to afflict the humane investigator, and hurry the benevolent reformer into a labyrinth of errour, who aims at destroying prejudices quickly which only time can root out, as the public opinion becomes subject to reason. An ardent affection for the human race makes enthusiastic characters eager to produce alteration in laws and government prematurely. To render them useful and permanent, they must be the growth of each particular soil, and the gradual fruit of the ripening understanding of the nation, matured by time, not forced by an unnatural fermentation. [*Short Residence*, 1795]

FINIS

Recipients of Letters

Eliza (Elizabeth Bishop) and **Everina Wollstonecraft** were Mary's younger sisters. Eliza was married soon after their mother's death, but when she became severely depressed following the birth of a daughter, Mary took it upon herself to spirit her away from the husband she believed had caused the condition. From then on, Mary spent a great deal of time and emotional energy in trying to find respectable positions for all her younger siblings.

Gilbert Imlay, five years Mary's senior, was born in New Jersey, fought in the Revolution, and worked as a surveyor in Kentucky before leaving, under a cloud, for London. In 1792-93 he wrote two popular books on America before moving on to Paris, where he met Mary through mutual friends. After their breakup, he reneged on child support. Little is known about his later life.

William Godwin, an intellectual and political guru as a result of his *Enquiry into Political Justice*, was three years Mary's senior but had had little romantic success (not for want of trying) prior to their meeting. Within the year after her death, he published his *Memoirs of the Author*, as well as four volumes of *Posthumous Works*, including the letters to Imlay.

FRIENDS AND ACQUAINTANCES

Jane Arden was a girlhood friend who also became a teacher and governess.

Ruth Barlow and her husband met Mary in London, and renewed their acquaintance when both turned up in Paris. Barlow was one of Gilbert Imlay's associates in the attempt to arrange for the import of goods from Sweden.

George Blood was the youngest brother of her dearest friend, Fanny. After the latter's death in childbirth, Mary continued to take a maternal interest in George, giving him advice and helping him out of scrapes till his irresponsible behavior became too much for her to deal with.

George Dyson was an intellectual and would-be artist in Godwin's circle.

Henry Gabell met Mary when she was en route to her post as governess in Ireland. Later, she stayed with him and his wife in Warminster, where he had become headmaster of a school.

Mary Hays was a writer and avid correspondent who unsuccessfully pursued Godwin for a while.

Joseph Johnson was the radical London publisher who took Mary under his wing and made it possible for her to be the first woman to earn a living as a writer and translator. He published all her books.

William Roscoe was an attorney and political liberal who so admired *Vindication* that he wrote verses in Mary's honor and arranged to have her portrait painted.

Bibliography

MARY WOLLSTONECRAFT'S WRITINGS AND LETTERS

NOTE: The [*abbreviated titles*] are used in the text to identify the sources of the quoted passages.

[*Education of Daughters*] *Thoughts on the Education of Daughters: with Reflections on Female Conduct, in the More Important Duties of Life.* London: J. Johnson, 1787.

[*Original Stories*] *Original Stories from Real Life; with Conversations, Calculated to Regulate the Affections, and Form the Mind to Truth and Goodness.* London: J. Johnson, 1788.

[*Revolution*] *An Historical and Moral View of the Origin and Progress of the French Revolution, and the Effects it has produced in Europe.* London: J. Johnson, 1794. In Janet M. Todd, Ed. *A Wollstonecraft Anthology.* Bloomington: Indiana University Press, 1977.

[*Rights of Men*] *A Vindication of the Rights of Men, in a Letter to the Right Honourable Edmund Burke; occasioned by his Reflections on the Revolution in France.* London: J. Johnson, 1790.

[*Rights of Woman*] *A Vindication of the Rights of Woman;
with Strictures on Political and Moral Subjects.* Vol.
I [all printed]. The Second Edition. London: J.
Johnson, 1792.

[*Short Residence*] *Letters Written during a Short Residence in
Sweden, Norway, and Denmark.* London: J. Johnson,
1796.

[*Posthumous Works*] *Posthumous Works of the Author of A
Vindication of the Rights of Woman.* In four volumes.
London: J. Johnson, 1798.

Collected Letters of Mary Wollstonecraft. Ralph M.
Wardle, Ed. Ithaca and London: Cornell University
Press, 1979.

NOTE: The letters to Imlay have been reprinted many
times since their publication by William Godwin in
the *Posthumous Works*. Prior to the Wardle collection,
they were issued, with new prefaces, in 1879 by C.
Kegan Paul (London), who sparked a revival of
interest in Wollstonecraft, and in 1908 by Roger
Ingpen (Philadelphia).

MAJOR BOOKS BY WILLIAM GODWIN

*An Enquiry Concerning Political Justice, and Its Influence
on General Virtue and Happiness.* London: Robinson,
1793. (This title was changed slightly in subsequent
editions.)

*Memoirs of the Author of A Vindication of the Rights of
Woman.* London: J. Johnson, 1798.

OTHER SOURCES

Anonymous. *A Defence of the Character . . . of the late Mary Wollstonecraft Godwin*, 1803. Quoted in H. R. James (see below), p. 167.

Bishop, Eliza Wollstonecraft. Letter to Everina, quoted in Sunstein (see below), p. 214.

Brailsford, Henry Noel. *Shelley, Godwin, and Their Circle*. New York: Henry Holt; London: Williams and Norgate, 1913.

Butler, Marion, and Todd, Janet, Eds. *The Works of Mary Wollstonecraft*. 7 vols. New York: New York University Press, 1994.

Catlin, George E. G. Introduction to *A Vindication of the Rights of Woman*. Everyman Edition. London: J. M. Dent & Sons Ltd.; New York: E. P. Dutton & Co. Inc., 1929.

Ferguson, Moira, and Todd, Janet. *Mary Wollstonecraft*. Twayne's English Authors Series. Boston: Twayne Publishers, 1984.

Flexner, Eleanor. *Mary Wollstonecraft: A Biography*. New York: Coward, McCann & Geoghegan, Inc., 1972.

Hagelman, Charles W., Jr., Ed. Introduction to *A Vindication of the Rights of Woman*. New York: W. W. Norton & Company, 1967.

Ingpen, Roger. Prefatory Memoir to *The Love Letters of Mary Wollstonecraft to Gilbert Imlay*. Philadelphia: Lippincott; London: Hutchinson, 1908.

James, H. R. *Mary Wollstonecraft: A Sketch*. Oxford University Press. London: Humphrey Milford, 1932.

Linford, Madeline. *Mary Wollstonecraft*. London: Leonard Parsons, 1924.

Marshall, Mrs. Julian. *The Life & Letters of Mary Wollstonecraft Shelley*. London: Richard Bentley & Son, 1889.

Paul, C. Kegan. Prefatory Memoir to *Mary Wollstonecraft: Letters to Imlay*. London: C. Kegan Paul, 1879.

Pennell, Elizabeth Robins. *Mary Wollstonecraft Godwin*. In Eminent Writers Series, John H. Ingram, Ed. London: W. H. Allen & Co., 1893.

Sapiro, Virginia. *A Vindication of Political Virtue*. Chicago & London: The University of Chicago Press, 1992.

Seward, Anna. From *Letters of Anna Seward*, quoted in Flexner (see above), p. 165.

Sunstein, Emily W. *A Different Face: The Life of Mary Wollstonecraft*. New York, etc.: Harper & Row, Publishers, 1975.

Todd, Janet M., Ed. *A Wollstonecraft Anthology*. Bloomington, London: Indiana University Press, 1977.

Tomalin, Claire. *The Life and Death of Mary Wollstonecraft*. London: Weidenfeld and Nicolson, 1974.

Walpole, Horace. From *The Letters of Horace Walpole*. Quoted in Tomalin (see above), p. 110.

Ward, A. C. *English Literature*. London: Longmans, 1958.

Wilson, Arthur M. Review of Claire Tomalin, *The Life and Death of Mary Wollstonecraft*. The New York Times Book Review, January 5, 1975.

She died in her prime, intellectual and physical, leaving to the daughter to whom she then gave birth a mingled inheritance of genius and sadness . . . Her opinions have become in many particulars the commonplaces of our own day, while she who was first to proclaim what is now held innocently was forgotten or assailed.

C. Kegan Paul, Prefatory Memoir,
Mary Wollstonecraft: Letters to Imlay, 1879